100 Ways to Create a Great Ad

Tim Collins

Laurence King Publishing

Published in 2014 by
Laurence King Publishing Ltd
361–373 City Road, London
EC1V 1LR, United Kingdom
T +44 (0)20 7841 6900
F +44 (0)20 7841 6910
enquiries@laurenceking.com
www.laurenceking.com

This book was produced by Laurence
King Publishing Ltd, London.

A catalogue record for this book is
available from the British Library.

ISBN: 978-1-78067-168-0

Design: Mucho
Picture research: Ida Riveros

Printed in China

CONTENTS

INTRODUCTION

A quick confession: when I was working as an advertising creative and found myself stuck on a brief, I would sometimes flip through awards annuals for inspiration. It wasn't that I wanted to steal ideas — honest. It was more that I noticed the same types of ad coming up again and again: some showed two different things combined into one; some showed objects that looked like other objects; some were written in a tone of voice that switched from the grand to the mundane.

I found that thinking about these different techniques could open up new ways into tricky briefs. Not always, of course, but often enough to make it worthwhile.

This book gives an overview of a hundred different approaches to creating an ad. They don't all work in the same way: some are rhetorical devices that have been around for thousands of years; some are visual techniques inherited from art and design; others have their roots in classic sales arguments. But they are all useful approaches that are worth considering one by one.

I hope this book can help to remind creatives of the variety of methods open to them. Certain techniques, such as visual similes and metaphors, are attempted a lot at the moment, while others, such as the devices used for witty headline writing, are under-used.

I also hope this book will be useful to the wide range of people who encounter creative ideas in their working lives. Marketing executives, account handlers and other professionals are often required to evaluate ads, and these brief introductions should provide them with a helpful framework.

Whether you're an industry professional or simply interested in why you see the same patterns repeated over and over again, this book should allow you to tell your mash-ups from your metaphors. And if you're stuck on the brief from hell, I hope it provides that moment of inspiration when you switch from staring out of the window with your feet on the desk to frantically scribbling on your notepad.

01

REVEALS

01 / Nike
The classic structure of the headline reveal. The first sentence sets up an assumption and the second contradicts it.

02 / Old Spice
'I'm on a horse.' This phenomenally popular Old Spice commercial ends with a visual joke known as the 'pull back and reveal'.

03 / The Guardian
This ad for *The Guardian* newspaper is a master class in reversing viewer assumption. We think the skinhead is attacking the businessman, then discover he's actually saving him.

A classic headline reveal can be seen in the Nike poster ''66 was a great year for English football. Eric was born.' We initially assume the ad is referring to England's only World Cup win. But we find it's actually referring to the birth of Eric Cantona, who played for Manchester United.

A similar technique in TV is known as 'pull back and reveal'. The viewer is led to believe they're seeing a particular situation, only to find out that they're looking at a totally different one. This can generate a quick visual joke. For example, we might think we're looking at a glamorous or idyllic environment and then discover we're seeing a mundane or squalid one.

The technique can also be used to more serious effect, as in the 'Points of View' ad for *The Guardian*. At first we think a skinhead is running away from someone. Then a different angle makes us think he's attacking a businessman. But a wide shot helps us understand he's actually saving the man from falling bricks.

Radio advertising is well suited to this sort of misdirection. An ad created by Ricky Gervais for the Prostate Cancer Charity features a doctor giving a man a rectal examination. Afterwards, the man asks, 'Does he have to be here?' We then hear the voice of a third man, who's been in the scene all along. This kind of 'radio reveal' can be a good way to generate surprise.

'66 WAS A GREAT YEAR FOR ENGLISH FOOTBALL. ERIC WAS BORN.

01

SMELL LIKE A MAN, MAN.
Old Spice

02

03

02

MASH-UPS

Mash-ups bring together incongruent images, genres and styles.

Mixing two very different things together can often create something new. The technique has been used in everything from Monty Python sketches to bootleg remixes of Slipknot and Justin Bieber to novels such as *Pride and Prejudice and Zombies*. Combining mismatched images can create strong print advertising. A poster for the *Financial Times* blended Richard Branson and Che Guevara to illustrate 'business revolutionaries'.

The technique can be used to generate surprising visuals. A Telefonica ad showed an Asian man with red hair to illustrate the claim, 'The lowest call rates to Japan and Scotland'. The Natural History Museum mixed images of children and explorers for their 'New recruits wanted' campaign.

TV and radio are perfect for mixing different genres and styles. The effect is often deliberately silly, as with the Heineken commercial that combined costume drama with action movie.

The incongruity can also be shocking. A radio ad for the charity Women's Aid described domestic abuse in the style of a Mills & Boon romance. A TV ad for children's charity the NSPCC combined slapstick animation with disturbing live action. A boy who is being attacked by his father is shown purely through animation until the very end, when we see him lying face down on the floor. The line was, 'Real children don't bounce back'.

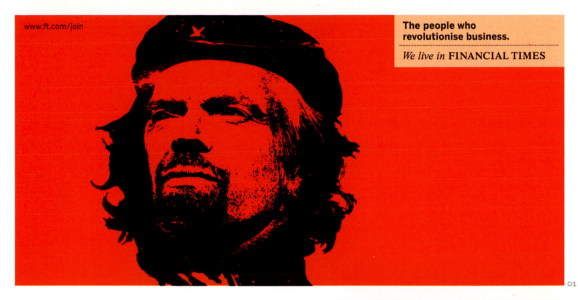

www.ft.com/join

The people who
revolutionise business.

We live in FINANCIAL TIMES

01

NATURAL
HISTORY
MUSEUM

ICE STATION
ANTARCTICA

NEW RECRUITS WANTED

Book now at **www.nhm.ac.uk/ice-station**
Booking fee applies ⊖ South Kensington
Opens 25 May

03

Associate Sponsor
Voyages
of Discovery

02

01 / **FT**
Mash-ups combine
two contrasting
visuals. Here, an icon
of communism is
mixed with an icon
of capitalism.

02 / **Natural
History Museum**
This campaign for
the Natural History
Museum mashed up
images of grizzled
explorers with those
of child visitors.

03 / **NSPCC**
'Real children don't
bounce back'. This
NSPCC ad combined
cartoon violence
with live action to
upsetting effect.

03

DOUBLE MEANINGS

Incredibly popular with copywriters, 'double meanings' are words or phrases that can be read in two different ways.

A famous British example is Saatchi & Saatchi's 1979 'Labour isn't working' poster for the Conservative Party. This three-word poster could be taken to mean both that the British workforce was unemployed and that the governing Labour Party was failing.

New York radio station WINS used the classic slogan 'You give us 22 minutes, we give you the world'. The station 'gives you the world' both in its commitment and in its international scope.

Some provocative campaigns use lines that could mean good or bad things about the brand. The UK online electrical retailer Dixons ran the line 'The last place you want to go'. While hinting at the snobbery some might feel about discount retailers, this also acknowledges that many people buy things cheaply online after spotting them in shops.

The positive connotation of the line outweighs the negative one.

Shocking or taboo double meanings can be playfully hinted at. An ad for Albany Life Assurance asked, 'Are you making plans for your wife's death?' and showed a knife, a pillow, some bleach and some pills.

Double meanings can also be a source of lewd humour. A campaign for the UK package holiday firm Club 18–30 was a master class in sexual innuendo, featuring such lines as 'Something deep inside her said she'd come again', 'Holiday forecast: Damp, followed by wet patches' and 'Wake up at the crack of Dawn (or Lisa, or Julie, or Karen …)'.

01 / Albany Life Assurance

Dark double meanings can grab attention. In this ad, the plans you should be making for your wife's death involve insurance rather than murder.

02 / Club 18–30

Smutty double meanings can be appropriate for 18–30-year-old fun-seekers. Other audiences might be put off by them, though.

03 / The Conservative Party

According to some, this double meaning was powerful enough to sway the result of the 1979 UK general election.

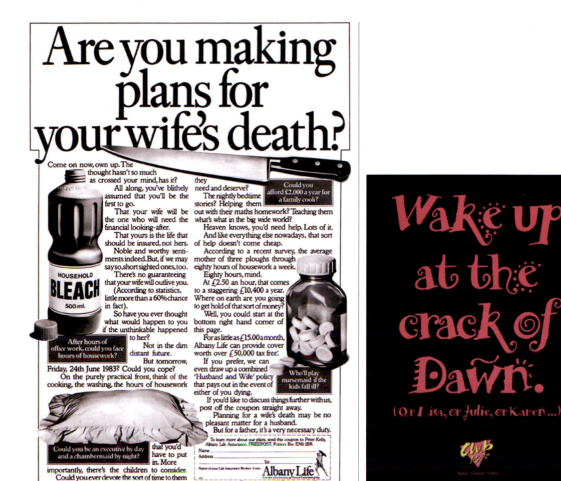

01

02

03

04

Although adored by young children and tabloid sub-editors, puns are generally disliked in modern advertising.

PUNS

It's worth clearing up exactly what is meant by 'pun'. Lines that exploit two different meanings of a word or phrase, such as those discussed in the last entry, can be considered puns. But this entry is about lines that substitute a word with one that sounds the same or similar.

Several famous endlines are based around puns, such as 'Nothing runs like a Deere' for John Deere tractors, 'See America at see level' for Amtrack, 'I think therefore IBM', 'Did you MacClean your teeth today?' and 'If you want to get ahead, get a hat' for the British Hat Council. These lines are now regarded as classics, but familiarity can reduce the groan factor. Let's not forget that the name of the biggest band of all time, the Beatles, is also a terrible pun.

A few decades ago, campaigns based around puns were celebrated by the industry. An award-winning poster campaign for Walls sausages by CDP featured the lines 'Porky and Best' (a play on *Porgy and Bess*), 'Pinky and Porky' (a play on *Pinky and Perky*) and 'I'm meaty, fry me' (a reference to the notorious 'I'm Margie, fly me' campaign for National Airlines). Even the hallowed *Economist* poster campaign featured such pun executions as 'Think someone under the table'.

Puns haven't been shown much love by juries since then, though some executions, like 'Roger more' for Durex condoms and 'Mom, Dad … I'm Gaelic' for Finnegans Irish Amber, have sneaked into annuals.

Puns can be direct and entertaining. But they're also very easy to write. It seems odd for a client to pay an agency fee for something they could quickly come up with themselves. But while linguistic puns have fallen out of favour, visual puns are still widely admired, as detailed in the next entry.

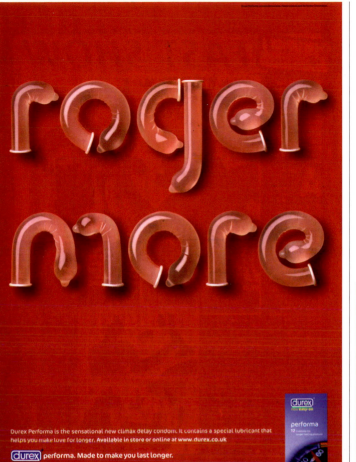

Durex Performa is the sensational new climax delay condom. It contains a special lubricant that helps you make love for longer. Available in store or online at www.durex.co.uk

durex performa. Made to make you last longer.

01

Think someone under the table.

The Economist

02

01 / Durex
This cheeky condom poster puns on the name of James Bond star Roger Moore, 'roger' being one of the many sexual euphemisms in English.

02 / The Economist
Puns are unfashionable now, but were once used in the very best campaigns. Even *The Economist*'s campaign featured a couple.

03 / Finnegans Irish Amber
This pun was originally created for Finnegans Irish Amber by Fallon Minneapolis, but now survives on novelty St Patrick's Day T-shirts.

"MOM, DAD... I'M GAELIC."

FINNEGANS IRISH AMBER. AS IRISH AS IT GETS.

03

Visual puns bring metaphorical figures of speech to life.

05

VISUAL PUNS

01 / Fiat
Visual puns can make
for quick, clean posters.
This Fiat ad plays on
the phrase 'a wolf in
sheep's clothing'.

02 / Harvey Nichols
This poster for the
Harvey Nichols sale
brings the phrase
'catfight' to life in
an entertaining way.

03 / Skins
An uneven playing field.
Visual puns bring to life
the bizarre imagery
we take for granted in
everyday expressions.

Everyday language is full of metaphors we take for granted. Showing the literal meaning of such phrases creates a visual pun. It's a familiar technique from broad comedy, as when Ted Striker in *Airplane!* says, 'the shit's gonna hit the fan', and we cut to some actual excrement splatting on to a fan.

Visual puns can be relied on for a quick gag. A poster for the UK listings magazine *Time Out* showed a candle being burnt at both ends. An Australian ad for the sportswear brand Skins featured an uneven playing field, implying that the clothing gives you an unfair competitive edge. A poster for Fiat cars showed a wolf disguised as a sheep.

As in the Fiat example, visual puns can sometimes communicate the benefit without the need for an explanatory line. This creates clean, simple ads that can stand out among cluttered competition.

Sometimes big-budget TV ads are built around a single visual pun. A Super Bowl ad for the IT company EDS brought the phrase 'herding cats' to life by showing cowboys leading cats across desert plains.

Similar to the visual pun, the 'stealth pun' is a visualized phrase that's hidden to give an extra layer of humour. For example, a Charmin toilet tissue campaign featured animated bears in woods. This is an obvious reference to the rhetorical question 'Do bears shit in the woods?' Watch out for stealth puns if you're a client buying work from an ad agency.

The new Fiat 132.

FIAT

01

THE
HARVEY NICHOLS
SALE

02

03

06

A visual metaphor communicates a benefit by showing something different with the same quality.

VISUAL METAPHORS

01 / Nike
Tennis star Pete Sampras was renowned for his explosive serve, as brought to life in this visual metaphor for Nike.

02 / Samsonite
Your luggage goes through hell. A metaphor that could have seemed familiar is brought to life with great craft.

03 / News channel 1
News coverage that places you right in the action. Some visual metaphors are so simple they work without any copy.

Visual metaphor is sometimes regarded as a primitive technique, and it's not hard to find examples of ads where cheetahs are used to represent speed, or tailors are used to represent 'bespoke solutions'. But it can make for simple, impactful communication when used well.

The classic 'Cages save lives' poster for Volvo showed a cage protecting a diver from sharks. A TV execution developed the metaphor by dubbing traffic noises over the sharks. It was a compelling argument to buy, and gave the ads a dark, murky tone that was unusual for the sector.

When they're executed well, visual metaphors can be so simple they don't need any words at all. An award-winning ad for Thailand's News Channel 1 replaced a camera with a viewer to show how their coverage places you at the centre of the action.

Some visual metaphors stand out due to the sheer amount of care that goes into crafting them. JWT Shanghai's ad for Samsonite shows the torture that luggage endures on an aircraft in contrast to the heavenly treatment passengers enjoy. The idea that luggage goes through hell could have been executed in a clichéd way, but the ad brought the metaphor to life in intricate detail.

"Advantage Sampras" 01

02

03

07

A visual simile, or visual echo, presents an object to look like something else. It's a popular way of creating print executions that often impresses awards juries.

VISUAL SIMILES

01 / Greenpeace
The holes in a torn piece of paper resemble trees in this ad for Greenpeace. Sometimes unusual cropping helps create visual similes.

02 / Tate Gallery
'A conker noticed after a visit to the Tate'. This art gallery campaign used a series of visual similes.

02 / John West
The rims of a tin can resemble water ripples in this John West poster.

Sometimes visual similes can be created by clever photography or cropping. The 'Don't forget it's a diesel' poster for Volkswagen shot a petrol pump to look like an elephant. A recycling ad for Greenpeace cropped a torn piece of paper so that the holes looked like trees. A poster for John West tuna with the line 'Straight from the sea' cropped an opened tin lid to make it resemble a wave.

Good creatives develop an eye for the visual echoes they encounter in everyday life. Some, like the faces that can be imagined on the fronts of cars, are obvious and have been overused. But it takes a highly tuned visual sense to spot the similarity between a petrol pump and an elephant or a ripped piece of paper and a row of trees.

Visual similes are often used for stand-alone ads, but it's also possible to create a campaign out of them. A campaign for the Tate Gallery with the line 'Minds open from 10am' showed a series of objects that looked like other things, including a conker that looked like an eye, beansprouts that looked like swans and a vine that resembled a human figure.

01

Recycle paper. Save trees. **GREENPEACE**

A conker, noticed after
a visit to the Tate
Minds open from 10am.

TateGallery

02

nothing but fish

03

JOHN WEST

08

ANALOGY

Analogies compare a product or brand to something more familiar that people can relate to.

It's worth remembering that comparisons can be made between words as well as pictures. Some analogies that might seem contrived as visuals can be turned into engaging headlines with good writing.

A straightforward form of advertising analogy makes a comparison between using the product in question and another enjoyable experience. DDB's classic Polaroid ad showed a product demonstration with the line 'It's like opening a present'. It was a simple and credible comparison to something everyone has experienced, and it helped to establish Polaroid cameras as a separate category from traditional photography.

Analogies can also be used to create concise headlines that make convincing sales arguments. Consider Wild Turkey's 'There are less expensive bourbons. There are also thinner steaks and smaller cars.'

Longer analogies can be sustained for more complex issues. An ad for the Continental Bank by Fallon McElligott read, 'Let's say the foot is your company, the banana is a change in interest rates, and the floor is extremely hard.' The copy refers back to the comparison at the end, giving the ad a pleasing circularity: 'There'll still be bananas in the world. But at least you won't be stepping on them.'

01 / Polaroid

The analogy between peeling back a Polaroid and opening a present is a convincing one, and evokes the fun and excitement of the product.

02 / Wild Turkey

Analogy is used for a convincing sales argument in this ad for Wild Turkey bourbon by Angotti Thomas Hedge.

03 / Continental Bank

Analogies can bring a dry subject matter to life. Here Fallon McElligott uses one to inject humour into the world of business banking.

POLAROID®

It's like opening a present.

Polaroid Color Pack Cameras start at under $60.

01

There are less expensive bourbons. There are also thinner steaks and smaller cars.

WILD TURKEY

8 years old, 101 proof, pure Kentucky.

02

Let's say the foot is your company, the banana is a change in interest rates, and the floor is extremely hard.

The economy can be accused of many things. Predictability is probably not one of them.

This economic fickleness can place your company in a rather vulnerable position. As you charge boldly into the future, eyes on the horizon, even a fairly minor fluctuation in interest rates can sneak up on you and bring your company to its knees.

Or to some even humbler portion of its anatomy.

The same thing can happen, of course, if exchange rates or commodity costs decide to dance a little jig.

Clearly, something should be done to deal with this threat. At Continental Bank, we suggest financial risk management.

In brief, risk management allows your company to specify exactly how much rate variation you're willing to tolerate. If rates rise or fall beyond

the limits you've specified, you're protected.

Whether the rate in question is the prime or Eurodollar, yen or deutschemark.

Beyond the obvious peace of mind it offers, financial risk management confers numerous other benefits.

It controls your cost of funds. It allows you to budget your interest expense with greater confidence. It prevents unforeseen depletion of your capital. On the whole, it permits you to do business in a much more orderly fashion.

Risk management is a relatively recent arrival on the financial scene, but it is already being heralded as the ideal mix of prudence and opportunity. It accords well with our philosophy—which is to bring our customers the most innovative, most effective financial tools we can find, develop or invent.

To learn more about how risk management can help your company, talk to a Continental banker at (312) 828-5799. There'll still be bananas in the world. But at least you won't be stepping on them. **Continental Bank** A new approach to business.

03

09

OMISSION

01 / Wonderbra
Some ads leave gaps in the visual and leave readers to work out what's going on. Here the product gives us all the clues we need.

02 / Nike Arsenal
Omitting words or letters can also produce good executions. This Nike ad celebrated English football team Arsenal's year without a Premier League loss.

03 / Fisher-Price roller skates
The visual of this wonderfully simple Fisher-Price ad omits something the headline leads us to expect.

A classic Fisher-Price press ad featured a boy standing alone on the right of a picture. The headline was, 'Which of these three kids is wearing Fisher-Price anti-slip roller skates?' Rather than showing the slapstick image of a child falling over, the ad invites us to imagine it, making for a much funnier execution.

A Brazilian ad for a push-up bra also used unusual cropping. It looks as though we are seeing a queue of people with a large gap. It's only when we read the product name that we understand what's really going on.

The principle of omission works just as well on TV, as in the Alka-Seltzer ad where we see two men adrift in a boat. The ad cuts to one of the men alone. The voiceover is, 'Alka-Seltzer. For when you've eaten something you shouldn't have.'

Omitting letters or words can also make for clever advertising. In 2004, the English Premier League team Arsenal completed an entire season without defeat. Their record of wins, draws and losses could be written as WWWWDDWWWDWWWD DWDWWDWWWWWWWWWDWDW DDDWW. Nike ran this as a poster, also omitting the 'L' from the name of the club.

01

02

Which of these three kids is wearing Fisher Price anti-slip roller skates?

When we set ourselves the task of producing a brand new roller skate, we took a long, hard look at conventional skate designs.

And then threw them all away. Then we started again. From scratch.

We asked literally hundreds of children, and their parents, exactly what they wanted in a roller skate.

Between us, we came up with something unlike any other skate on the market.

Instead of having an angular metal construction, it's made of rounded, virtually indestructable plastic.

We replaced laces and buckles with simple velcro straps. We gave them flexible toe grips so they fit either foot.

We designed a built-in catch which adjusts their size, doing away with the need for spanners or keys.

But most importantly we developed a unique way of adding to their stability and safety.

We designed a switch which prevents the front wheels from spinning backwards.

And yet for all their simplicity, it's ideas like these that are the reason why Fisher Price have already sold nearly a million pairs of skates in America.

So it seems that while our customers tend to stay upright once they're in our skates, they're virtually falling over themselves to buy a pair.

Fisher-Price

03

10

MINIMALISM

Advertising has always aspired to quick, single-minded ideas. But how far can simplicity go? How many elements can you remove and still communicate?

Many print executions dispense with headlines and endlines. A Malaysian campaign for Jeep used shapes representing different types of terrain such as a husky dog and a camel. The outline of the car was created in the overlap of the images.

Some ads cut out the logo as well as the line. In seventies and eighties Britain, agencies responded to restrictions on cigarette advertising with minimalism and surrealism. A poster for Silk Cut by M&C Saatchi showed just a piece of purple silk with a slit in it. It was a visual pun on the brand name that drew attention through its very simplicity.

Perhaps the most extreme example of minimalism in print was 'The Missing Piece' for *The Economist*. The magazine's red-and-white poster campaign had been running for over two decades, and was so established that the logo could be replaced by the outline of a jigsaw piece.

Minimalism has been used in broadcast too. A cinema ad for clothing brand FCUK showed nothing but a white screen for 30 seconds, followed by the caption 'FCUK Advertising'. It was an ingenious way of standing out from noisy, fast-cutting competition.

A 2007 German radio ad for Zippo lighters featured the sound of someone trying to use a disposable lighter before binning it, followed by a Zippo lighting up in a way that evoked the brand name. Even in radio, wordless minimalism is possible.

LOW TAR As defined by H.M. Government
DANGER: Government Health WARNING:
CIGARETTES CAN SERIOUSLY DAMAGE YOUR HEALTH

01

01 / **Silk Cut**
Cigarette advertising responded to restrictions with enigmatic minimalism in the seventies and eighties, as in this classic visual pun for Silk Cut.

02 / **Jeep**
This campaign communicated Jeep's all-terrain proposition using simple outline shapes. An image of the car is created by the overlap.

03 / **The Economist**
'The Missing Piece' for *The Economist*. About as far as you can take advertising minimalism without running a blank poster.

02

03

11

RHYME

01/Haig
Rhyming a word with the brand name is a traditional way of writing an endline. This one ran for over 40 years.

02/Nissan
'You can with a Nissan'. The rhyming endline takes the place of a headline in this magazine ad for the Japanese motor company.

03/Heinz
Rhyme is an ingredient in many classic endlines. 'Beanz meanz Heinz' was named as the greatest slogan of all time in *Creative Review* magazine.

Using rhyme is a simple way to make headlines and endlines memorable.

Endlines often rhyme words with the brand name, as in 'Don't be vague, ask for Haig', 'You can with a Nissan', 'We all adore a Kia-Ora', 'Don't just book it, Thomas Cook it' and 'For mash get Smash'.

Other lines turn the product benefit into a memorable rhyme, as in Zanussi's 'The appliance of science', 'A Mars a day helps you work, rest and play', 'Please don't squeeze the Charmin' and 'It takes a licking and keeps on ticking' for Timex.

Sometimes spelling is altered to emphasize rhyme, as in 'Milk's gotta lotta bottle', 'Beanz meanz Heinz' and 'WotalotIgot' for Smarties.

Rhyme can be used to give TV and radio ads a poetic quality. Leo Burnett's 'Favourites' ad for McDonald's features the actor David Morrissey reading a voiceover about 'Gothy types and scoffy types and like-their-coffee-frothy types'.

Some agencies have even commissioned poets to write rhyming voiceovers, as in the 2002 Prudential ad written by Nick Toczek. It featured lines such as, 'They moan, we groan, but re-invest / In those who've grown and flown the nest'.

01

02

03

12

ALLITERATION

Alliteration is the repetition of a particular sound in a series of words or phrases, especially consonants at the beginning of words, as in the tongue twister 'Peter Piper picked a peck of pickled peppers'.

Alliterative phrases tend to be memorable, which is why they're common in brand names, headlines and endlines. Many well-known brand names have used alliteration, from Coca-Cola to Dunkin' Donuts to PayPal. Some slogans alliterate the consonant in a brand name, as in 'Greyhound's going great' and 'My Goodness, My Guinness'.

Others play on different consonants, such as Jaguar's 'Don't dream it, drive it' and Country Life's 'You'll never put a better bit of butter on your knife'. A subgenre of alliterative endline uses three adjectives that begin with the same letter, as with Fila's 'Functional … Fashionable … Formidable …'.

If long lists of alliterative words seem a little cheesy, there's always the option of a pairing just a couple in a line, as with 'The daily diary of the American dream' for the *Wall Street Journal*. And there's always the tongue-in-cheek option of alliteration that doesn't quite work but is still memorable. A campaign for the umbrella brand Knirps ran in the early eighties with the line 'You can break a brolly, but you can't knacker a Knirps'.

Alliteration is used in headlines too, as in Ben & Jerry's 'Crammed full of cream'. Alliteration is incidental to the main idea here, but it helps to give the execution a pleasingly friendly tone.

01

01/Marmite
'My Mate Marmite'. Many famous lines have been created by repeating the first letter of the brand name.

02/Guinness
'My Goodness, My Guinness'. Alliteration has been used in countless memorable lines, although the technique can seem old-fashioned now.

03/Ben & Jerry's
Alliteration is sometimes overdone, but it's used sparingly and effectively in this execution of the 'Homemade Ltd' campaign for Ben & Jerry's.

My GOODNESS
My GUINNESS

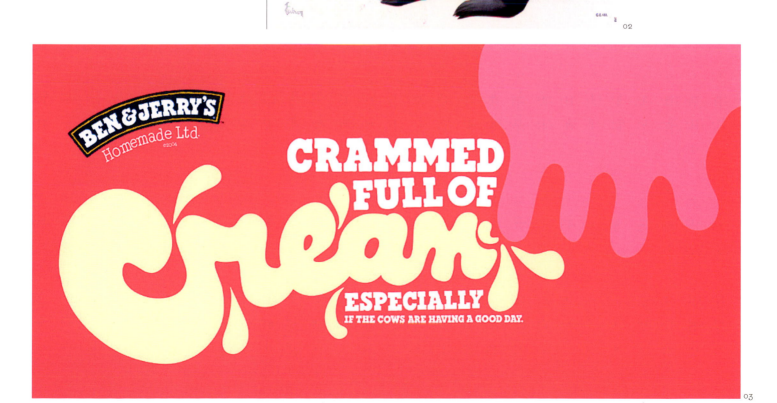

02

03

13

QUESTIONS

01 / Got Milk?
'Got Milk?' Questions have been in many of advertising's most famous endlines. This line is so familiar from parody and imitation that it's easy to forget how good it is.

02 / Freedom Foods
'Does it matter how they lived?' The headline raises a thought-provoking question and the copy sets out a persuasive argument.

03 / ABC
Questioning headlines can also work without body copy, as in this humourous campaign for US TV network ABC.

Writing headlines and endlines as questions is a traditional way of engaging readers. It's often best to aim for thought-provoking questions rather than ones that can be easily answered and dismissed.

A traditional way of structuring press ads is to pose an interesting question in the headline and answer it with body copy. AMV's ad for the charity Freedom Foods asked, 'They're dead. So does it matter how they lived?' The headline invites you to consider your stance on animal rights before the copy suggests that you pay slightly more for ethically farmed meat. It makes for a tone that's calmly persuasive rather than hectoring.

Question headlines can also work without copy, as with *The Economist*'s 'Would you like to sit next to you at dinner?' and ABC's 'If TV's so bad for you, why is there one in every hospital room?'

Some of advertising's most famous endlines have been posed as questions. The UK newspaper *The Independent* was launched with the line 'It is. Are you?' A sophisticated question about how the media forms our political opinions was posed in four small words.

Goodby Silverstein's campaign for the California Milk Advisory Board introduced the most famous questioning endline of all. 'Got milk?' is so familiar now it's difficult to remember what a good job it does. Rather than explaining the benefits of milk, the line simply prompts us to try and remember if we have enough in the fridge. And we all know how annoying it is to run out.

got milk?

01

Does it matter that cattle have fresh straw to lie on not bare concrete?

Does it matter that hens have room to forage and a quiet box to lay their eggs in?

Does it matter that sows should be able to root and explore instead of being tied to one spot?

We know it matters to the animals. The question is, does it matter to you?

If it does, look for the 'Freedom Food' mark in your supermarket.

A new venture initiated by the RSPCA, it aims to give farm animals five basic freedoms:

1. Freedom from fear and distress.

2. Freedom from pain, injury and disease.
3. Freedom from hunger and thirst.
4. Freedom from discomfort.
5. The freedom to behave naturally.

With Freedom Food there'll be no battery hens. No tethered pigs. No overloaded cattle trucks.

The farmers, hauliers and abattoir owners have to agree to very strict conditions.

Freedom Food assessors visit them regularly and the RSPCA does unannounced spot checks to keep them up to the mark.

To begin with, you can find our stickers on a range of pork, bacon,

ham and eggs in Tesco and the Co-op.

Soon we're extending the scheme to beef, lamb, poultry and meat products such as hamburgers and lasagne, in more shops.

Some may cost a little more, it's true.

But any profits Freedom Food makes will help fund RSPCA farm animal welfare research.

And if you can find it in your heart to pay the extra, one day all animals raised for food will lead happier lives. If you can't, they won't.

Sorry to leave the problem on your plate.

FREEDOM FOOD RSPCA MONITORED

They're dead. So does it matter how they lived?

02

If TV's so bad for you, why is there one in every hospital room?

abc

03

14

THE RULE OF THREE

01 / Sure
Headlines and endlines often use the rule of three. This deodorant ad lists three examples of things that make you sweat.

02 / American Floral Association
Posters and press ads often show three things side by side. In this formula, a visual exaggeration is delivered in three stages.

03 / Cancer Research
A more emotive take on the principle, this ad dramatizes the statistic that lifetime risk of cancer is one in three.

Three, as hip hop group De La Soul pointed out, is the magic number. Things that are grouped into threes are somehow more inherently satisfying than things that are grouped into other numbers. From the three little pigs to the genie's three wishes to the three ghosts in *A Christmas Carol*, threes abound in stories and literature.

In advertising, the rule of three can be employed visually and in copy. Showing three things side by side is an enduringly popular way to lay out landscape posters and double-page press ads. An example is the 'Exactly how mad is she?' poster for the American Floral Association. A comic exaggeration is built up in three stages, leading to an enjoyable punchline.

The same principle can be used for a more serious tone of voice. An ad for the charity Cancer Research showed three children sitting side by side with the words 'Lawyer', 'Teacher' and 'Cancer' above them. It was a very simple way to communicate the grim statistic that lifetime risk of cancer is one in three.

The rule of three is also useful in headlines, which often list three things. As outlined in the entry on 'Bathos', the tone can often switch from serious to silly for the third one. But a headline can also be a more straightforward list of three things, as in an ad for Sure deodorant.

Endlines often list three words that describe the brand, as with Jaguar's 'Grace. Space. Pace'. But this technique can seem a little stale, especially in business-to-business advertising, where generic words like 'excellence', 'quality' and 'reliability' are thrown carelessly together.

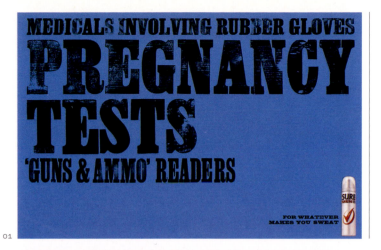

01

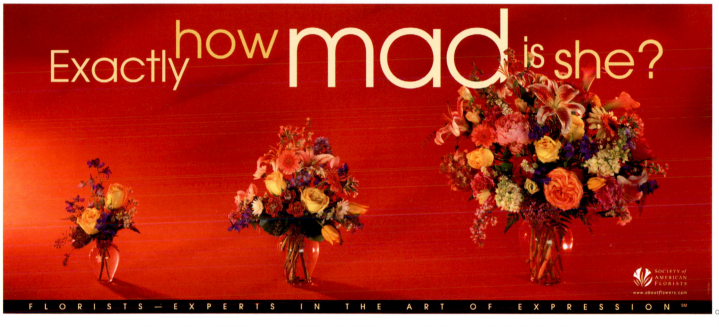

02

03

15

CONTRASTING PAIRS

01 / Marston's
This tongue-in-cheek campaign stirred up the rivalry between supporters of the English and Australian cricket teams with contrasting pairs.

02 / The Mail on Sunday
The Mail on Sunday This endline sets up a contrasting pair in just five words.

03 / Vinçon
This ad for a design shop in Barcelona plays on the double meaning of 'stink' to construct a contrasting pair.

A useful tool when writing headlines, endlines and copy is to group sentences or phrases into contrasting pairs. It's a method that's used in famous quotations such as Mae West's 'It's not the men in your life that matters, it's the life in your men.'

Contrasting pairs are good at highlighting differences between a product and its competitors, or a target market and another group. Marston's Beer Company sponsor the English cricket team, and they ran a campaign of headlines in this format, poking fun at the Australian rivals during an Ashes series. Executions included 'England has history. Australia has previous', and 'We're English, we brew beer. You're Australian, you serve it.'

Sometimes the same phrase is repeated with a minor change, as in 'How to keep food you can't finish from becoming food you can't identify' for Sterilite food containers, and 'Just because it stinks on the inside doesn't mean it has to stink on the outside' for the design shop Vinçon.

Endlines often condense a similar contrast into just a few words. Clairol's classic line 'Does she or doesn't she?' uses the technique, as does 'No FT, no comment' for the *Financial Times*, 'A newspaper, not a snoozepaper' for the *Mail on Sunday* and 'Think globally, act locally' for Friends of the Earth.

01 drinkaware.co.uk

A Newspaper.
Not a Snoozepaper.

02

JUST BECAUSE IT STINKS ON THE INSIDE DOESN'T MEAN IT HAS TO STINK ON THE OUTSIDE.

PEDAL WASTE BIN 24.90€

VINÇON
DESIGN·SHOP

03

16

LISTS

01 / Citroën
Presenting copy as a list can make it easy for readers to digest. This Citroën ad is a list of jokes about other car names.

02 / Rosendorff
This ad for the jewellers Rosendorff lists the entire history of the universe from one big bang to another.

03 / Millets
A family camping holiday is evoked through a tent inventory in this long-copy ad for outdoor equipment chain Millets.

Creatives are often advised to make body copy flow seamlessly from the headline to the conclusion, to avoid it sounding like a list. But lists are sometimes used on purpose.

A press ad for the Citroën 2CV Dolly made a virtue of its odd name with a list of lines that punned on other car names. The wordplay was so engaging it kept you reading.

An ingenious ad for the Australian jewellers Rosendorff used the list form to give a history of the universe from the Big Bang to a type of big bang that might occur after 'man gives diamond to woman'.

Some ads spoof formats such as ingredients or instructions to tell us about a brand. MCBD's press ad for Millets uses a tent inventory to describe a family camping holiday.

The list can be a useful format in radio and TV too. The award-winning 'Litany' ad for British newspaper *The Independent* took the form of a long list of things we're told not to do, concluding with a shot of the paper itself and the words 'Don't read. Don't buy'.

01

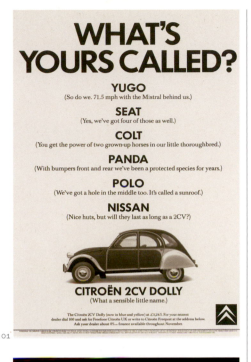

WHAT'S YOURS CALLED?

YUGO
(So do we. 71.5 mph with the Mistral behind us.)

SEAT
(Yes, we've got four of those as well.)

COLT
(You get the power of two grown-up horses in our little thoroughbred.)

PANDA
(With bumpers front and rear we've been a protected species for years.)

POLO
(We've got a hole in the middle too. It's called a sunroof.)

NISSAN
(Nice huts, but will they last as long as a 2CV?)

CITROËN 2CV DOLLY
(What a sensible little name.)

The Citroën 2CV Dolly (now in blue and yellow) at £3,245. For your nearest dealer dial 100 and ask for Freefone Citroën UK or write to Citroën Freepost at the address below. Ask your dealer about 0%™ finance available (throughout November).

02

Big Bang

Sun Forms

Planets Orbit

Earth Cools

Rock Crushes

Diamonds Form

Amoeba

Dinosaurs

Man

Man Digs Up
Diamonds

Rosendorff Man
Buys Diamonds

Man Gives
Diamond To Woman

Big Bang

ROSENDORFF

03

THE MILLETS DELUXE FAMILY TENT PACK. £149.99

INCLUDES

1 three-room, four-person tent	3 shouts of 'Are we there yet?'
4 sleeping bags	4 games of Pooh-sticks
2 roll mats	5 burnt sausages *(inedible)*
1 double airbed	1 burnt sausage *(sort of edible)*
8 gobsmackingly beautiful sunsets	1 knot-tying session
5 blackbird wake-up calls	2 tree-climbing sessions
2 glorious days without a phone signal	3 rolling-down-the-hill sessions
1 cowpat incident	30 seconds of feeling really dizzy
3 scary campfire stories	1 pair of pants lost in your sleeping bag
1 rather dull campfire story	1 river crossing
4 pees behind trees	2 waterlogged wellies
1 grasshopper solo	1 fruitless search for kindling
16 hot chocolates	1 plastic plate melting on the barbecue
1 brother-on-sister assault *(dead leg)*	1 intimate moment *(interrupted)*
5 games of 'I spy'	3 chats with a friendly farmer
1 sister-on-brother assault *(Chinese burn)*	6 long country walks
3 rude awakenings by some very loud snores	1 morning spent nursing blisters
1 bizarrely smelly hedgerow	1 large, unidentified creepy-crawly
2 messy grass stains on your knees	3 ladybirds
1 attempt to wash clothes in a river	8 picnics
5 butterfly chases	1 stubbed toe
1 'plastic plate versus paper plate' debate	1 peat bog *(really boggy)*
15 dandelions	5 shooting stars
1 trillion dandelion seeds	½ an earthworm
3 atishoos	6 games of football *(boys only)*
2 occasions when you trip over the guy ropes	1 snail in the shower
1 zap by an electric fence	8 lazy afternoons
3 marshmallows stuck on a stick	2 games of rounders *(girls only)*
5 failed attempts to identify Orion's Belt	15 nasty nettle stings
1 huge moan about not having a hairdryer	1 search for dock leaves
7 eerie noises in the middle of the night	3 hissy fits
6 splashes in puddles	1 scream of 'Where's the loo roll?'
4 sploshes	1 dead rabbit discovery
2 splishes	3 hills you run down very fast
20 minutes making daisy chains	15 skims of a stone *(personal best)*
40 matches that won't light	1 hole accidentally burnt in your fleece
1 dawning realisation the matchbox is wet	1 mole trying to burrow under the tent
1 cry of 'Ouch! Blasted thistle!'	1 stumble over a stupid rock
8 sheep that won't be stroked	9 beautiful dewy mornings
2 hours spent making clouds look like faces	25,063 cubic metres of fresh air
14 campfire sing-alongs	
1 campfire sing-along *(in tune)*	
10 muddy fingernails	
2 minutes spent reading a map upside down	

Simple stories with satisfying conclusions can make entertaining ads.

17

STORYTELLING

01 / Social work
This UK recruitment campaign for social workers used the techniques of graphic novels to tell stories in print advertising.

02 / Levi's
Urban myths can be adapted into entertaining narratives. This Levi's ad used one about a boy who buys a packet of condoms from his date's father.

03 / John Lewis
This John Lewis ad misdirects the viewer before delivering a satisfying, sentimental pay-off.

Telling a story with a successful beginning, middle and end is difficult enough in a two-hour movie. Making one work in a TV ad is incredibly difficult, though ads that manage it are often very popular.

Volkswagen's 2011 Super Bowl spot featured a young boy dressed as Darth Vader attempting to control objects by holding his arms out and using 'the Force'. In the end, he seems to succeed in starting the car, but we learn that his dad is actually using a remote control. It's an enjoyable pay-off that's set up with brilliant economy.

Misdirection is important in storytelling. In the John Lewis ad 'The Long Wait', a boy anxiously counts down the days until Christmas. At the end we discover that it's giving rather than receiving he was actually looking forward to.

Some ads adapt jokes or urban myths, which are often simple stories with satisfying conclusions. An urban myth with its roots in forties America involves a teenage boy who buys a packet of condoms from the pharmacy before a date. When he knocks on the door of the girl's house, her father turns out to be the pharmacist he saw earlier. Levi's adapted this for the hugely successful 'Drugstore' ad in the nineties.

Stories can be told in print through long copy or multiple images. A recruitment campaign for social workers in the UK used the techniques of graphic novels to relate case studies.

winter.
the last season.

people are proud

but Errol's not afraid of death.

as he tells you he's had a good life.

TOTAL
Marriage 1
Children 4
Jobs 3
Years 82

a good innings he says.

only one more thing he wants.

a dignified walk to the pavilion.

his family far away

called to say he can't manage alone.

but the emotional support, handrails and help you organised kept Errol at HOME like he wanted.

to die at home in his own bed.

out.
they were big things you did. because they made death a small thing to Errol.

wherever he's gone

There'd Better BE BLOODY CRICKET

people can be fascinating, mystifying, rewarding. social work is work with people, it's that simple and that complicated. to find out more about training to be a qualified social worker call for a career booklet on 0845 604 6404, or visit www.socialworkcareers.co.uk (minicom: 0845 601 6121)

social work
it's all about people.

01

GENERAL STORE

Watch pocket created in 1873. Abused ever since.

Levi's
501. The Original Jean.

02

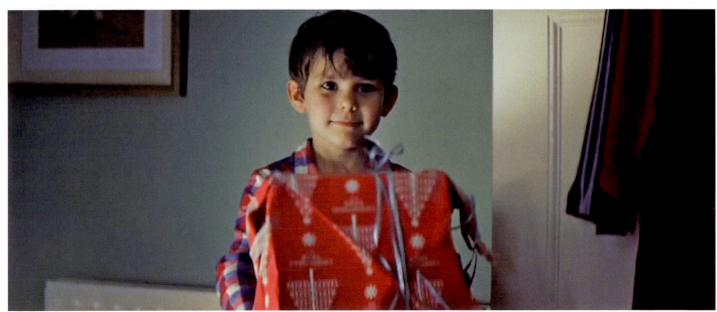

03

18

CONSEQUENCES

01 / Budget car rental
Slapstick consequences of decisions can be a source of humour, as in this campaign for Budget.

02 / Land Rover
Showing the effects of a product can lead to simple, lateral executions, as in this Land Rover ad.

03 / Ouch! plasters
Print advertising can use images with obvious consequences. There's no need to explain what would happen if a child used this sharp tin lid as a toy flying saucer.

Print advertising can tell a story in a single image with a clear outcome. An ad highlighting the 'energy-absorbing door padding' of the Volkswagen Golf showed a cyclist hurtling towards an open door and looking the wrong way.

A press ad for Ouch! children's plasters showed a discarded tin lid with the caption 'flying saucer'. There was no need to explain what would happen if a child used this sharp object as a toy, or where the product would come in.

A similar type of ad shows the consequences of using the product but not the product itself, as with Land Rover's 'Birds' ad.

TV ads can portray unusual or unexpected consequences. A PlayStation 2 ad in the 'Third Place' campaign showed a fawn stepping on to a road as a car approaches. When the two collided, it was the car rather than the animal that was damaged.

A campaign for Budget car rental by Cliff Freeman and Partners showed staff brainstorming new offers. One execution showed a woman suggesting free aromatherapy candles in all cars. It then cut to a car in which everyone, including the driver, was asleep. The car drifted over into the opposite lane and crashed.

01

02

Flying Saucer

03

19

SEQUENCES

01 / Heineken
It's often said that posters should be reduced to single images, but this Heineken campaign used sequential images to entertaining effect.

02 / MTV
'Sex is no accident'. These wordless comic strips set up unlikely slapstick events to promote condom use.

03 / Dunn & Co
This ad for menswear retailers Dunn & Co could have been reduced to a single image, but this might have been less engaging.

Creatives are often told that print ads should work in single images, and that press and poster executions with multiple images would be better off as TV storyboards. But there are many examples of entertaining print ads that use multiple images.

The 'Heineken refreshes the parts other beers cannot reach' campaign from the seventies and eighties included posters of consecutive images that worked like comic strips. They showed Mr Spock's ears straightening out, a halo appearing above J. R. Ewing from *Dallas* and King Harold protecting his eye from an arrow attack.

A press ad for British menswear retailers Dunn & Co, with the headline 'Success doesn't always go to your head', showed a man's stomach expanding over three photos. It's the sort of ad that could be reduced to a single image if you wanted to trim away the fat (no pun intended). But the multiple images added to the comedy.

A more recent campaign run by MTV to promote condoms used comic strips to tell wordless slapstick stories. Each ad showed an unlikely series of events that led to people ending up in sexual positions. The line was, 'Sex is no accident. Always use a condom.'

20

HOMAGES

Advertising has always been influenced by wider cultural trends, but the issue of where homage ends and plagiarism starts is a difficult one.

Paying homage to movie scenes has long been popular, but taking inspiration from short films, video art and music promos is more controversial. In 1997, British director Mehdi Norowzian accused the Irish agency Arks of copying his short film *Joy* for a Guinness ad. He pursued the claim in court, and was ultimately unsuccessful, but the case brought to light the issue of how close homages should be to their inspirations.

Honda 'Cog', a 2003 ad that set up a perfect chain reaction between the parts of an Accord, received a rapturous reception from the industry. Some pointed out it was similar to *The Way Things Go*, a short film by Swiss artists Peter Fischli and David Weiss, and the ad's makers were open about the influence.

Sony Bravia's 'Balls', which showed hundreds of multicoloured rubber balls bouncing down a hill in San Francisco, attracted acclaim a couple of years later. Soon a similar clip from *The David Letterman Show* emerged online. Whether the idea was directly inspired by it or not, you can at least see the value of a big-budget remake. The *Letterman* segment was a throwaway gag, while 'Balls' is a brilliantly crafted spot.

Idea borrowing became a hot topic in the age of viral clips and video-sharing sites. Almost every time an ad is posted on YouTube now, the comments section fills up with accusations of plagiarism. Sometimes they're a bit of a stretch, but sometimes they're convincing.

The answer for agency creatives is simple. Try the 99 other ways to create an ad detailed in this book before you resort to YouTube to find something to 'homage'.

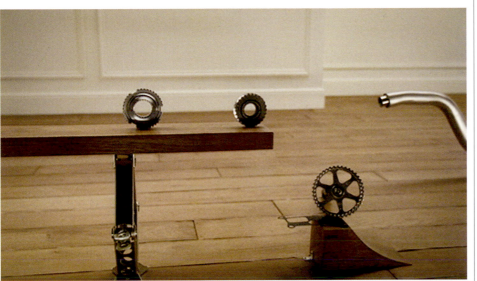

01 / Honda
The makers of this Honda ad said it was made as an open homage to the short film *The Way Things Go*.

02 / Guinness
Director Mehdi Norowzian claimed this Irish Guinness ad was too heavily influenced by his short film *Joy*. The case brought the issue of advertising plagiarism into the spotlight.

03 / Sony Bravia
A similar clip from *The David Letterman Show* did the rounds following the success of this Sony Bravia commercial.

01

02

03

'Borrowed interest' ads use existing properties, such as characters from books, film and TV.

21

BORROWED INTEREST

01 / VW
This VW ad from DDB New Zealand used the associations of Superman to create a simple and clever ad.

02 / Marmite
This famous Marmite campaign showed people and things that divide opinion, such as Chelsea FC's manager Jose Mourinho.

03 / Barclaycard
This Barclaycard ad makes witty reference to fictional characters Dr Jekyll and Mr Hyde.

Ads using borrowed interests are often discouraged in ad agencies, as they're seen as piggybacking on someone else's creativity. Some people would regard adapting a popular TV comedy sketch into an ad as no different from choosing a sports team for a brand to sponsor. But borrowed interest can be used very inventively.

A DDB New Zealand press ad for the Golf R32 showed the VW logo in the colours of the Superman logo. It proved that borrowed interest can be a route to the kind of wordless minimalism that modern creative departments aspire to.

Another clever use of colour came in the launch campaign for the Simpsons Ride at Florida's Universal Studios theme park. Lisa Simpson's usual yellow skin was turned a sickly green to match her queasy expression. The other executions were Ned Flanders praying and a close-up of Homer's scalp, showing one of his two hairs blowing off.

A campaign for Gatorade Kids recreated famous sporting events using children. Executions included Pelé's first World Cup win and a classic Michael Jordan basketball shot.

All these ads use the associations of existing properties to create quick, clever visuals, and prove that there's more to borrowed interest than hiring TV comedians to rehash sketches.

01

02

You either Love it or hate it.

03

Are you worried that your Barclaycard will bring out the worst in you?

We've heard people say that they're too sensible to use their Barclaycard as a credit card.

They say that if they did, they wouldn't use it sensibly.

But this reasonable concern is stopping a lot of people getting as much out of their money as they could.

For instance, it's a simple matter to budget for fixed commitments like a mortgage, but what about the unexpected?

Like when your car goes on strike the day before you go on holiday? Or when the kids need new clothes to go back to school.

And the house can't face another winter without a new coat of paint.

At such times you'll find your Barclaycard, far from turning you into a spendthrift, can help you eke out your money with almost miserly enthusiasm.

But your Barclaycard is more than something you save for a rainy day.

There's probably something you want to buy.

Something with a hefty price tag.

You could save up for it, of course. But will your savings ever catch the soaring price?

It makes sense to buy now.

And the simplest way is with your Barclaycard.

You won't waste time filling in H.P. forms and waiting for clearance. And with Barclaycard, you can vary the amount of each repayment.

But however easy it seems, we know a lot of people still worry about using credit.

The funny thing is, it's just these people, once they use Barclaycard, who get the most out of it.

Bills no longer strike terror into them.

They find it easy to buy most things they need.

It's almost as if using Barclaycard changes them into completely different people.

For further information, call at any branch of Barclays (in Scotland, any branch of the Bank of Scotland).

Or write to Barclaycard Chief Office, Department MA, Northampton NN1 1SG.

You don't have to bank with Barclays to have a Barclaycard.

22

Reversal shows people and things doing the opposite of what we'd expect.

REVERSAL

A good way of grabbing attention is to show people and things doing the opposite of what we'd expect. There have been countless ads showing children acting like adults, adults acting like children, men acting like women and women acting like men.

A famous example is Saatchi & Saatchi's 'Pregnant Man' for the Family Planning Association. To encourage more men to use contraception, it showed a pregnant man holding his bump with the line 'Would you be more careful if it was you that got pregnant?' And a clever 2007 poster for a Tide stain-removal pen showed a man with a shirt that was dirty except for the area where the pen had leaked.

Some brands use reversal as campaign strategy. The 'How Refreshing! How Heineken!' campaign featured a pigeon with droppings on its head, and 'Have a break, have a Kit Kat' featured pacifist versions of war-mongering robots the Daleks.

In headline writing, an established phrase can be switched around to create a surprising new meaning. The phrase 'The doctor will see you now' was reversed to 'The patient will see you now, doctor' for Bupa, a private healthcare firm.

A Metropolitan Police ad highlighting the number of security cameras on London transport showed a mugger nicking a camera. The headline was, 'A camera nicking a mugger'.

A Scottish anti-smoking ad showed a cigarette with the line 'It gets through thirty a day', a witty reversal of the way people describe how much they smoke.

A long-running *Economist* campaign also used reversal in many headlines, including 'Great minds like a think', 'Shine and rise' and 'Trump Donald'.

"THE **PATIENT** WILL SEE YOU NOW **DOCTOR**"

0800 600 500

BUPA

01

02

01 / Bupa
Reversing figures of
speech can produce
surprising headlines,
as in this UK ad for
a private healthcare
company.

02 / Tide
Depicting the opposite
of normal situations
can be a clever way to
demonstrate a product,
as with this stain-
removal pen.

03 / UK Health Council
The pregnant man.
Reversals can produce
arresting visuals,
as in this 1970 ad
encouraging men to
use contraception.

Would you be more careful if it was you that got pregnant?

**Anyone married or single can get advice on contraception from the Family Planning Association.
Margaret Pyke House, 27-35 Mortimer Street, London W1 N 8BQ. Tel. 01-636 9135.**

The Health Education Council

03

23

DISPLACEMENT

01 / ITV
Displacement puts people or things into inappropriate environments, as in this poster for coverage of British football competition the FA Cup.

02 / Reebok
Transplanting a character into an incongruous environment can lead to entertaining TV work, like this series for Reebok.

03 / New Zealand Transport Agency
Displacement can also put across a serious message, as in this poster for the New Zealand Transport Agency.

A poster for ITV coverage of the FA Cup, where major and minor football teams meet, showed a milkman tackling a footballer. The headline was, 'The FA Cup. Where all men are equal.' It was a quick visual that encapsulated the appeal of the competition.

The contrast between place and person can lead to outrageous humour. A DDB Paris poster for Live Poker showed a black man attending a Ku Klux Klan meeting. The line read, 'Become the King of Bluff'.

Such incongruities can be explored in more detail on TV. Reebok's 'Terry Tate' campaign featured an NFL linebacker hired to police an ordinary office. Tate aggressively berates workers for failing to refill the coffee pot, neglecting to recycle and talking outside of designated break times. Sometimes the contrast between person and place is so strong it can stretch to multiple vignettes.

The effect of displacement can be serious as well as comic. A poster campaign for the New Zealand Transport Agency showed crash scenes where the cars were replaced with beds. The line was, 'Sleep before you drive'.

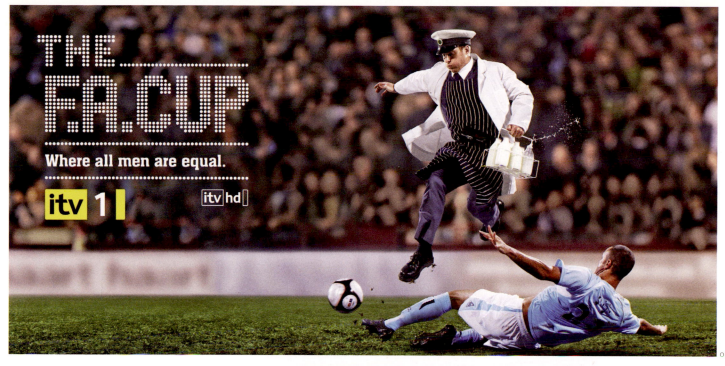

THE F.A.CUP

Where all men are equal.

itv 1   itv hd

01

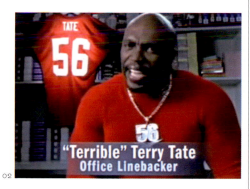

TATE
56

"Terrible" Terry Tate
Office Linebacker

02

Land Transport NZ and NZ Police
New Zealand Government

Sleep before you drive

03

24

DISRUPTION

01

An effective way of grabbing attention can be to disrupt the conventions of a medium. It's quite a common technique in press advertising to try and make it look as though an ad or product is somehow bursting through the page or crashing into the type of nearby articles. It might often be slightly overdone, but there are always inventive variations to be found, like the Johnnie Walker logo marching through the magazine barcode.

Ogilvy and Mather's campaign for Volkswagen was a clever take on the disruptive layout. To promote the company's range of environmentally friendly cars, they donated a portion of each press ad to non-profit eco-focused organizations, creating small-space ads-within-ads that partly obscured the product shot.

Lots of ambient ads and special-build posters could be regarded as disrupting outdoor media, but UK bitter brand John Smith's managed it with conventional printed posters. The ads seemed to capture the moment when a new poster is being plastered over an old one, but were deliberate comic juxtapositions of different tones of voice.

Countless TV ads have attempted to disrupt the medium. A 2000 UK ad for Heineken seemed to show an entire commercial break on fast forward until it reached a shot of a man enjoying a pint. It was an effective in-joke at a time when many viewers were watching programmes on VHS tape and forwarding through the ads.

It's all about giving a little bit back. **Eco-conscious BlueMotion technology.**

Das Auto.

02

03

25

CONTRADICTION

Deliberate contradiction can be a useful advertising technique. It's especially popular in print advertising, when a headline can be used to directly contradict the information a visual gives us.

A very famous example of the technique from art is René Magritte's painting *The Treachery of Images*, which shows a pipe alongside the words 'Ceci n'est pas une pipe' (This is not a pipe). The technique has been used a lot in art, often as a reference to Magritte or a comment on art itself.

In advertising, the technique is sometimes used to exploit the dominance of visual information. A classic DDB ad for tyres showed a car that had skidded off the road and crashed into a tree, alongside the headline 'A little drop of rain never hurt anybody'. The casual tone of the headline is overpowered by the attention-grabbing visual, and it's clear what we're meant to take out of the ad.

A famous anti-smoking ad from the American Cancer Society showed a haggard woman taking a drag from a cigarette above the headline 'Smoking is very glamorous'. This ad is using the technique in a humorous way, and like a lot of comedy, it contrasts the glossy myth with the ugly truth.

A more complex take on the device was used in a Saatchi & Saatchi campaign to recruit nurses. The ads were case studies demonstrating that nursing is both difficult and rewarding. In one of them, a woman is shown making an aggressive hand gesture alongside the headline 'For weeks no response. Then a positive sign.' The copy explains that when a patient is withdrawn, even an eruption of aggression can be a positive breakthrough.

01 / The Rain Tyre
'A little drop of rain never hurt anybody'. The headline battles the visual and loses in this ad for safe tyres.

02 / American Cancer Society 'Smoking is very glamorous'. A contradiction between the visual and the headline can be used humorously.

03 / Nursing
Contradictions can be a simple way of communicating complex ideas. If a patient is withdrawn, an aggressive outburst like this can be a positive sign.

01

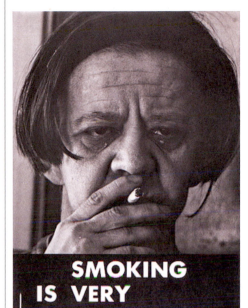

02

03

26

Repeating words and visuals can be used to surprising effect.

REPETITION

01 / Save the Children
'My mom's going to kill me'. Repeating the exact same words can bring out a surprising double meaning of a familiar phrase.

02 / Harvey Nichols
Repeating visuals can also make for unusual ads. Here repetition gives an insight into the sacrifices fashion-lovers make to get what they want.

As described in the entries on Lists and Contrasting Pairs, ad copy sometimes repeats phrases and sentence structures with minor changes. But it can also repeat exactly the same words over and over again, often to bring out an ironic double meaning.

An ad for the charity Save the Children repeated the phrase 'My mom's going to kill me' next to the head and stomach of a pregnant teenager, bringing out the grim double meaning of a common phrase. The line at the bottom of the page read, 'One condom saves both lives'.

Positive Thinking magazine used the technique for comic effect on a subscription insert, which is hardly a medium that screams 'creative opportunity'. Both check-box options on the card read, 'Yes, I want a one-year subscription'.

Visuals as well as words can be repeated, of course. A UK press ad for the chic department store Harvey Nichols showed a pair of their 'must have' shoes followed by a month's worth of beans on toast. It was an intriguingly different layout, especially for fashion advertising, and a credible insight into the sacrifices clothes-lovers make.

01

January

02

27

HYPERBOLE

01 / Nike
Hyperbole can be used to make a point forcefully. Several of the athletes in this campaign underperformed at the 1992 Olympics, however.

02 / Altoids
This campaign for Altoids used hyperbolic headlines like 'Mints so strong they come in a metal box' and 'You might want to practice on other mints first'.

03 / Olympus
Shorter isn't always better. The headline of this Olympus camera ad gives us 38 words of comic exaggeration.

Advertising is infamous for manipulating the truth about products, but sometimes exaggeration is used for rhetorical purposes rather than to mislead consumers.

Hyperbole uses exaggeration to emphasize a point – often for comic effect – but it is not meant to be taken literally. A Nike poster for the 1992 Barcelona Olympics featured Ukrainian pole-vault favourite Sergey Bubka alongside the line 'Spanish air traffic control has been notified'. Sadly, Bubka failed to win a medal at the games, so air traffic control didn't have much to worry about.

An ad highlighting the powerful zoom of an Olympus camera showed what appeared to be a close-up of actress Sandra Bernhard with the headline 'Take one more shot of me and I'm going to cross that street, jump over that fence, run through that wood, swim that river, climb to the top of that mountain and ram that camera down your throat'. Proof that shorter isn't necessarily better when it comes to headlines.

Further proof comes from a T-shirt created in Singapore to promote *The Economist*. The old slogan 'My dad went on holiday and all I got was this lousy T-shirt' is spun into a hyperbolic description of wealth: 'My dad read *The Economist* and all I got was this lousy tee shirt, a penthouse apartment in New York, two Ferraris, an eighty foot yacht, my own private jet and an island retreat in the Caribbean'.

SPANISH AIR TRAFFIC CONTROL HAS BEEN NOTIFIED.

01

"Take one more shot of me and I'm going to cross that street, jump over that fence, run through that wood, swim that river, climb to the top of that mountain and ram that camera right down your throat."

Whoever said the camera never lies was, to put it bluntly, lying. And there's no bigger liar than the Olympus Superzoom.

Its 55-120mm lens tells the massive whopper that you're right in the thick of the action when you're actually a safe distance away.

And when, like the charming Ms Bernhard here, your subject is more likely

to respond with something stronger than "cheese" you'll find the Superzoom's other features come in handy.

For instance, a high speed recording action captures any fast moves. And when that mouth starts, it really motors.

By re-distributing the camera's weight we have also improved its balance and minimised any camera-shake. So your hand

remains steady even if your pulse isn't.

But if you do get near enough to enjoy a filthy look, the flash makes sure it won't be coming from a pair of red eyes.

In fact, no less than four different flash modes adjust automatically as you get further and further away from your subject.

Throw in an ultra compact, light weight and weatherproof design and we

think you'll agree it makes quite a neat little package. Which, to be frank, is more than you'll have if Ms Bernhard were ever to get hold of you.

OLYMPUS SUPERZOOM 120

03

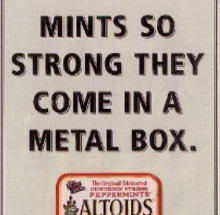

MINTS SO STRONG THEY COME IN A METAL BOX.

The Original Celebrated
CURIOUSLY STRONG
PEPPERMINTS
ALTOIDS

THE CURIOUSLY STRONG MINTS

02

28

*Comic visual exaggeration
can bring a touch of
cartoonish absurdity
to advertising.*

VISUAL HYPERBOLE

In advertising, comic exaggeration is used with images as well as with words. Visual hyperbole is a particularly popular technique in print advertising. Product benefits are depicted in a deliberately over-the-top way, often with cartoonish absurdity.

A very famous example of visual hyperbole is the eighties ad for Maxell cassettes that featured a man getting blasted by the sound from his speakers. In this heightened reality, the sound is so powerful it blows the man's hair and tie, and topples over his lampshade and martini glass. The image became a pop culture icon, and has been parodied by everyone from *Jackass* to *Family Guy*.

Visual hyperbole can lead to simple, wordless communication. A 1979 ad for Victory V lozenges parodied René Magritte's painting *The Son of Man* to show a figure who's head has been blown off by the strength of the sweets. It was a daringly wordless ad in an era when long headlines and copy were still the norm.

Visual hyperbole can be especially effective when you're dealing with tangible propositions like size, strength and durability. A press ad in VW's 'Tough new Polo' campaign showed a car door so strong it could bend a metal pole. Obviously, Volkswagen weren't claiming their cars could really do this, and it's unlikely that anyone tried it and complained to the Advertising Standards Authority when they smashed their door. Visual exaggerations are a useful form of shorthand that's easily understood by audiences around the world.

01

01 / **Victory V**
An early example of
wordless communication
that channelled surrealist
painter René Magritte
to dramatize the power
of Victory V lozenges.

02 / **Nikon**
'The widest lens
in its class'. Visual
hyperbole exaggerates
product features in
a way we're not meant
to take literally.

03 / **Maxell**
This example of visual
hyperbole became a
pop culture classic, and
was still being parodied
decades after it ran.

The widest lens in its class.

02

AFTER 500 PLAYS OUR HIGH FIDELITY TAPE STILL DELIVERS HIGH FIDELITY.

If your old favorites don't sound as good as they used to, the problem could be your recording tape.

Some tapes show their age more than others. And when a tape ages prematurely, the music on it does too.

What can happen is, the oxide particles that are bound onto tape loosen and fall off, taking some of your music with them.

At Maxell, we've developed a binding process that helps to prevent this. When oxide particles are bound onto our tape, they stay put. And so does your music.

So even after a Maxell recording is 500 plays old, you'll swear it's not a play over five.

IT'S WORTH IT.

29

UNDERSTATEMENT

Advertising has a reputation for making bold exaggerations about products, so it might be surprising to consider understatement as a creative technique. But it can be a useful method of engaging an audience.

Understatement is a device used in literature, film and everyday speech, and involves saying something that's technically accurate but unexpectedly flat. In *The Wizard of Oz*, Dorothy Gale finds herself in a fantastical Technicolor world full of bright flowers and munchkins. Instead of saying, 'What the hell is this place?', she says, 'I've a feeling we're not in Kansas anymore.' It's a brilliant bit of screenwriting that's passed into everyday speech.

Understatement in headlines can be used to create a contrast with a visual. An ad about climate change showed the devastating effects of a drought in Niger with the headline 'Sorry to bother you, but would you mind turning the thermostat down a degree?' An apologetic, casual tone rather than a sincere charity-ad voice is a surprise here. And surprise is important for a modern audience suffering from 'compassion fatigue'.

Understatement has been used to create memorable endlines, including 'Does exactly what it says on the tin' for the wood-dye manufacturer Ronseal. Rather than spouting endless claims about effectiveness, the campaign told us that Ronseal's quick-drying wood varnish could varnish wood and dry quickly. It was a distinct, no-nonsense tone of voice that has been much imitated since.

Carlsberg's 'Probably the best lager in the world' was a clever twist on big advertising claims that managed to sidestep regulations. But it proved that understatement doesn't always translate. The company had to drop the slogan when it launched a worldwide campaign in 2003, as international focus groups thought the line was criticizing the product.

01

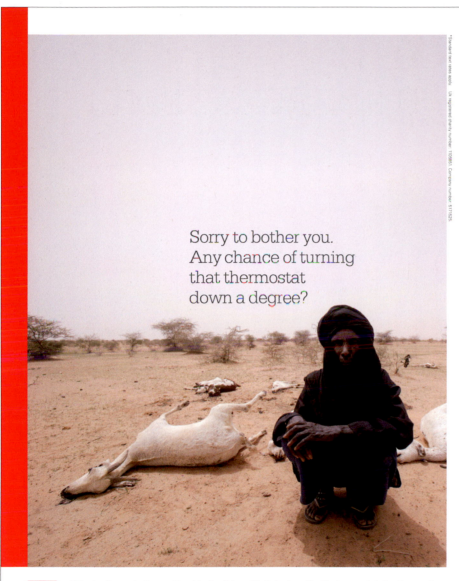

Sorry to bother you.
Any chance of turning
that thermostat
down a degree?

*Standard text rates apply.   UK registered charity number: 1105851. Company number: 5171525.

christian **aid** Climate change isn't some threat to the future. It's today's reality. Environmental disasters, such as droughts in Niger, are wrecking people's lives with more and more frequency. And it's going to get worse. Want to do something about it? Good, we need people like you. Visit our website to see how the actions of you and your workplace can change the world for the better. Or text CLIMATE1 to 84880 for an 'Actions' poster.* Climate changed. Let's get to work. **www.climatechanged.org**

02

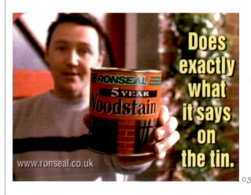

Does
exactly
what
it says
on
the tin.

www.ronseal.co.uk

03

01 / Carlsberg
The humorous insertion of the word 'probably' in this endline skirted advertising regulations and inspired a campaign that ran for three decades.

02 / Christian Aid
The visual leads us to expect a hard-hitting headline, so the casual tone of the line takes us by surprise.

03 / Ronseal
'Does exactly what it says on the tin'. We're used to endlines for products like this making big claims about effectiveness, so this down-to-earth tone stood out.

30

COMPARISON

01 / VW
'Put life in perspective'. Side-by-side comparisons can be used as much for smart, lateral strategies as for comparing cleaning products.

02 / Mexican Red Cross
In this appeal for cornea donors, 'before' is written in braille – a clever twist on an old formula.

03 / Rolling Stone
This 'Perception and reality' campaign for *Rolling Stone* magazine pitted the icons of the sixties and the eighties against each other.

Side-by-side comparison is sometimes associated with unsophisticated, old-fashioned advertising. 'Before and after' shots are used for baldness cures, domestic cleaners and anti-dandruff shampoos. But like any other technique, comparison can make for engaging advertising if used well.

Some ads riff on the 'before and after' convention. An appeal for corneal donors on behalf of the Mexican Red Cross featured the word 'before' in embossed braille and the word 'after' in regular type.

Visual comparisons can be used to make more sophisticated points than the effectiveness of carpet cleaners. A campaign for Volkswagen South Africa showed large things such as the giant redwood tree and Angel Falls next to tiny things such as 'your alarm clock' and 'your office water cooler'. The line was, 'Put life in perspective.'

Fallon's 'Perception and reality' campaign for *Rolling Stone* aimed to convince advertisers that the magazine's readership consisted of sophisticated eighties yuppies rather than pot-smoking sixties hippies. It did this with a series of stark side-by-side comparisons that have been much imitated since.

Press ads sometimes use consecutive pages to make a comparison. A famous example is an ad for the UK Health Education Council, which ran to raise awareness about AIDS when the disease first came to public attention. One page showed a photo of a woman with the line 'If this woman had the virus which leads to AIDS, in a few years she could look like the person over the page'. The photo overleaf was exactly the same.

The Angel Falls.

Put life in perspective. **Touareg**

AFTER

DONATE YOUR CORNEAS
National Transplant Center. www.cenatra.gob.mx

Perception.

Reality.

If you still think a Rolling Stone reader's idea of standard equipment is flowers on the door panels and incense in the ashtrays, consider this: Rolling Stone households own 5,199,000 automobiles. If you've got cars to sell, welcome to the fast lane.

Some ads use deliberately odd or enigmatic imagery.

31

SURREALISM

Occasionally ads that are regarded as surreal are merely conventional ads that don't communicate well. Perhaps a lateral strategy isn't linked to the product clearly enough, or a script is too overwritten to make sense in 30 seconds. But other ads are meant to be odd.

Restrictions on UK cigarette advertising in the seventies led CDP to create a series of surreal posters for Benson and Hedges, featuring the pack hidden among the Giza pyramids, hatching from eggs and locked in birdcages. The weirdness of the images inspired widespread public speculation about what the evil geniuses of advertising were trying to make them think.

Deliberately obscure visuals are sometimes used to reach younger audiences that would reject the conventional hard sell. Sony launched its PlayStation 2 console with the bizarre 'Third Place' campaign. The first TV spot was directed by David Lynch and featured a man walking down a corridor to meet himself, a mummy and a man with a duck's head.

Comic surrealism has led to many of the most famous TV ads of recent years, such as the Skittles 'Taste the rainbow' campaign. Executions featured a man eating Skittles with his beard, a girl growing Skittles in her eyebrows and a man who turns everything he touches into Skittles.

In the UK, an ad for Cadbury's chocolate that showed a gorilla playing a Phil Collins drum fill became a huge online hit. The brand's 'A glass and a half of joy' campaign aimed to create ads that were as enjoyable as the chocolate itself, and featured surreal executions such as racing airport trucks and children with dancing eyebrows.

01 / Cadbury
Fallon's 'A glass and a half of joy' campaign for Cadbury's chocolate featured surreal scenes of drumming gorillas and dancing eyebrows.

02 / Guinness
Guinness has a tradition of using surreal and dreamlike imagery, from white horses riding waves to fish riding bicycles

03 / Benson and Hedges
Government restrictions on cigarette advertising inspired surreal posters like this from Benson and Hedges in the late seventies.

01

02

MIDDLE TAR As defined by H.M. Government
H.M. Government Health Departments' WARNING: CIGARETTES CAN SERIOUSLY DAMAGE YOUR HEALTH

32

Shocking imagery can be an easy way to make an ad cut through. But it can backfire, leaving a brand or agency looking desperate for attention.

SHOCK

01 / Trojan
Pelvic power lifting. Risqué content was novel in the early days of online, but is no longer a formula for guaranteed viral success.

02 / Barnado's
A hard-hitting tone is common in charity advertising.

03 / Benetton
Photographer Oliviero Toscani created shocking posters such as this for clothing brand Benetton in the eighties and nineties.

Shock was traditionally the preserve of charity advertising. An ad by CDP for the Bhopal Medical Appeal showed a dead child in a shallow grave and the headline 'Thousands of our children were not so lucky. They survived.'

This hard-hitting tone was introduced into consumer advertising in the eighties when the fashion brand Benetton hired Italian photographer Oliviero Toscani to oversee their communication. Toscani's 'United Colors of Benetton' campaign featured striking, controversial images that were often unrelated to the product. Famous examples included a man dying of AIDS, a newborn baby still attached by its umbilical cord and the blood-stained clothes of a soldier who had died in the Bosnian War.

Shock has now become something of a convention in fashion advertising. A 2012 Harvey Nichols campaign showed models wetting themselves with excitement, and drew over 100 complaints from the public.

Shock tactics became much more common with the rise of online advertising and video sharing. In the early days of viral clips, it was assumed that risqué sexual content or slapstick violence would be enough to make consumers forward a clip. An agency called the Viral Factory set itself up to specialize in such ads, scoring hits with a campaign for Trojan condoms that showed sexual Olympic events such as pelvic power lifting, and a Ford Ka ad that showed a cat getting decapitated by a sunroof.

The novelty of such taboo-breaking clips soon wore off, but online still gives brands a chance to push their campaigns into risky areas.

01

02

03

33

Some ads aim for deliberate cheesiness to appeal to hip audiences.

IRONY

01

An ad for the tech website CNET showed a man with 'You' written on his T-shirt meeting someone with 'The Wrong Digital Camera' on his T-shirt. However, a man in a CNET T-shirt points him towards someone whose T-shirt reads, 'The Right Digital Camera'. It's the most laboured visual metaphor in advertising history, and the stilted performances and retro wardrobe make for an enjoyable spot.

Some ads flag their ironic intentions by casting celebrities – like Jean-Claude Van Damme, David Hasselhoff, Chuck Norris and Steven Seagal who have now spent longer as camp icons than they ever did as serious stars. A UK campaign for Asahi featured Z-list celebrities endorsing the lager in the style of Japanese ads.

The most successful ironic campaign ever is probably Bud Light's 'Real men of genius', which began as 60-second radio spots in the late nineties. The ads exaggerated the macho tone and earnest soft rock of eighties advertising and applied it to characters such as 'Mr All You Can Eat Buffet Inventor', 'Mr Boombox Carrying Roller Skater' and 'Mr Way Too Much Cologne Wearer'.

The danger of irony is that intentionally bad ads can look a lot like actual bad ads. But the 'Real men of genius' campaign shows how funny the tone can be if you get it right.

01/CNET
This CNET ad features
the world's least subtle
visual metaphor. But
the deliberately stilted
execution lets us know
the brand is in on
the joke.

02/Bud Light
'Real men of genius'.
This celebrated Bud
Light campaign shows
just how hilarious
ironic ads can be.

03/Cumberland Farms
Ironic ads often cast
cheesy celebrities such
as David Hasselhoff.

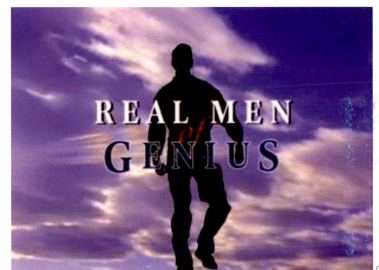

02

03

34

BATHOS

01 / **Millets**
Combine bathos with the rule of three and you get this headline formula. Two sensible benefits followed by a silly one.

02 / **Starbucks**
Abrupt changes of tone can be very funny on TV. The lyrics of the track in this Starbucks ad switch from macho to commonplace.

03 / **Mike's Hard Lemonade**
Switching tone of voice halfway through a headline can create funny executions, like this one for Mike's Hard Lemonade.

In TV advertising, a pompous speech or voiceover will often be deflated by a colloquial word or phrase. In a British ad for the alcoholic drink Campari, a foppish man asks a woman, 'Were you truly wafted here from paradise?' The woman replies, 'No, Luton Airport.' Her response became a popular catchphrase and was even turned into a hit single by the group Cats U.K.

In the 'Glen' spot by Starbucks, an office worker is followed around by the soft-rock group Survivor, who perform 'Eye of the Tiger'. The amended lyrics of the track, which originally featured in *Rocky III*, flit from manly to mundane: 'Burning the candle on the way to the top / He knows one day he just could become supervisor!'

Headlines often switch tone halfway through, as in the Mike's Hard Lemonade execution 'I watched you from afar in the park. You had me arrested.' Another popular headline format is to list two sensible details followed by a third, whimsical one. An ad for a Millets floral tent featured the line 'Delight Children. Impress Friends. Confuse Bumble Bees.' An ad for the Museum of Childhood read, 'Get here by train, by bus or by the power of Greyskull'.

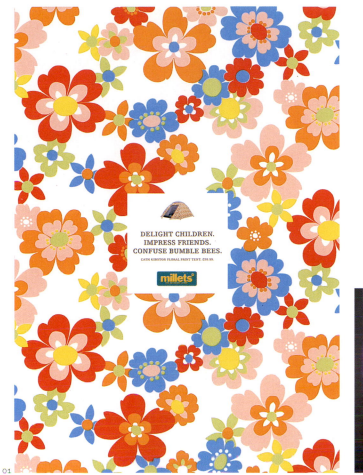

01

DELIGHT CHILDREN.
IMPRESS FRIENDS.
CONFUSE BUMBLE BEES.

CATH KIDSTON FLORAL PRINT TENT. £59.99.

millets

02

I watched you from afar in the park.

You had me arrested.

A hard day calls for a hard lemonade.   mike's hard lemonade   MAKE IT MIKE'S.

03

35

Lines that seem to contradict themselves can sometimes communicate a surprising truth.

PARADOX

01 / Stella Artois
This apparent contradiction exploits the colloquial term 'shout', which means 'turn to buy a round of drinks'. The 'reassuringly expensive' price of Stella Artois explains why you'd whisper it.

02 / Fiat
This endline is one of the most famous paradoxes in British advertising, partly because it featured in one of the first high-profile 'event' ads.

03 / PETA
'Imagine having your body left to science while you're still in it'. Paradoxes seem contradictory, but can communicate shocking truths.

Paradox is a common figure of speech in literature, from Shakespeare's 'I must be cruel only to be kind', George Bernard Shaw's 'What a pity that youth must be wasted on the young' and George Orwell's 'All animals are equal, but some are more equal than others.'

A paradox in an advertising headline can sometimes be explained by a visual. The classic PETA ad 'Imagine having your body left to science while you're still in it' plays on the apparent contradiction between leaving your dead body to research and still being alive. The visual reveals we're actually talking about experimentation on live animals.

The classic Stella Artois ad '"My shout," he whispered' is a paradox that makes sense in the context of the long-running 'Reassuringly expensive' campaign. Everyone wants to drink Stella, but no one wants to pay for it. So when it's your shout (your turn to pay for the drinks), you announce it very quietly.

Paradox can also be used in endlines, as in the classic 'Handbuilt by robots' for Fiat. The paradox was fitting for a campaign that depicted the apparently mundane world of robotic production lines as thrilling and dramatic.

"My shout," he whispered.

Every silver lining has a cloud.

There you are, in the midst of convivial company, laughing, joking, holding forth on the great issues of the day and pausing only to savour your Stella Artois.

And then the awful truth dawns.

It will soon be your turn to stand a round.

And not just any round, mark you: a round of Stella Artois, no less.

The beer that is brewed with the most fragrant of female hops.

The beer that is malted with the choicest of Europe's barley.

The beer that is matured not for the usual meagre 21 days, but for 6 long weeks.

The beer that, as a consequence, is eye-wateringly expensive.

If we are to maintain Stella's reputation for quality there is also nothing we can do to reduce the quantity of money you must part with.

We can, however, offer you a sound piece of advice.

When it is your turn in the chair, make sure you are sitting down.

Stella Artois. Reassuringly expensive.

01

Handbuilt by robots.

FIAT

The Strada.

02

Imagine having your body left to science ... while you're still in it.

peta2
FREE FOR ALL

03

36

SLANG

The Madison Avenue creative revolution of the sixties, which generated many of the creative strategies still used today, witnessed a great shift from formal to colloquial language.

The old guard of copywriters and art directors were gradually replaced with hip youngsters from Brooklyn and the Bronx. Traditional sales patter made way for street talk. A VW Beetle was famously described as a 'lemon'. A radio campaign for a brand of processed herring called Vita introduced a character called the 'herring maven', helping to popularize the Yiddish word for expert. And an ad for Horn and Hardart restaurant had the endline 'It's not fancy. But it's good.'

Since then, many campaigns have made good use of slang to communicate with a particular target audience. Droga5's 'Great Schlep' campaign used another Yiddish word to appeal to young Jewish voters in the 2008 US presidential election. 'Schlep' means a long, arduous journey, and the particular journey that was being encouraged was a visit to elderly relatives in swing states such as Florida. An online film showed comic Sarah Silverman urging viewers to schlep over to their grandparents and convince them to vote for Obama.

Colloquial words have been used in many classic endlines. A famous Pepsi endline from the seventies aped the fast-talking US radio DJs of the time with the mammoth 'Lipsmackinthirstquenchinacetastin motivatingoodbuzzincooltalkinhighwalk infastlivinevergivincoolfizzin Pepsi'.

01

You can so tell the people who like don't read The Economist.

01 / Pepsi
Various colloquialisms were incorporated into the 100-letter word that made up Pepsi's slogan in the early seventies.

02 / The Economist
Colloquialism isn't always used positively. This execution in *The Economist*'s 'White out of Red' campaign uses slang expressions to imply stupidity.

03 / The Great Schlep
In 2008, comic Sarah Silverman encouraged viewers to 'schlep' over to Florida and convince their grandparents to vote for Obama.

37

*Some facts are interesting
enough to make good headlines
on their own.*

KILLER FACTS

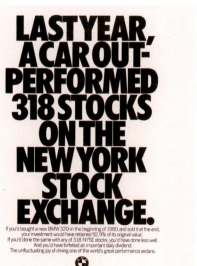

LAST YEAR, A CAR OUT-PERFORMED 318 STOCKS ON THE NEW YORK STOCK EXCHANGE.

If you'd bought a new BMW 320i in the beginning of 1980, and sold it at the end,
your investment would have retained 92.9% of its original value.
If you'd done the same with any of 318 NYSE stocks, you'd have done less well.
And you'd have forfeited an important daily dividend:
The unfluctuating joy of driving one of the world's great performance sedans.

THE ULTIMATE DRIVING MACHINE.

01

Copywriters are sometimes criticized for writing flat, straightforward headlines that present facts without any sort of rhetorical twist. But sometimes you'll come across a fact so compelling it doesn't need a twist.

In 1981, BMW ran an ad explaining that one of their cars had retained so much of its original value that it would have been a better investment than 318 stocks on the New York Stock Exchange. The creatives might have buried this in the copy and constructed a lateral headline or visual, but instead they made it the point of the ad. It showed a mature approach that seems rare now. The agency weren't drawing attention to themselves with clever visuals or complicated strategies; they were simply stating a compelling reason to buy.

Killer facts are often used well in charity and public service campaigns. A South African campaign for the Endangered Wildlife Trust highlighted the plight of endangered species such as the northern white rhino by printing photos of all the remaining individuals left on the planet. A shocking set of facts that didn't need to be embellished with the emotive tone of traditional charity advertising.

Factual headlines don't even have to be short if they're compelling enough. Cramer Saatchi's famous press ad for the Health Education Council was a 72-word description of what happens when a fly lands on your food.

Some creatives might feel they're not doing their job properly if they simply pass on facts they've read in a brief, but there are times when this might be the best creative choice of all.

YOU ARE LOOKING AT EVERY NORTHERN WHITE RHINO LEFT ON THE PLANET.

To save the last 8 visit ewt.org.za

ENDANGERED WILLDLIFE TRUST

01 / BMW
The BMW that retained its value better than most stocks. When you have a fact as compelling as this, why not make it the focus of your ad?

02 / Endangered Wildlife Trust
Every northern white rhino left on the planet. Sometimes all charity campaigns have to do is present us with the shocking truth.

03 / Health Education Council
A compelling 72-word account about what happens when a fly lands on your food for the Health Education Council by Cramer Saatchi.

38

SELF-AWARENESS

As consumers have become wise to advertising techniques over the last few decades, ads themselves have begun to acknowledge their own conventions.

This approach has its roots in the honest, witty tone of voice established by Doyle Dane Bernbach in the sixties. The agency's famous Volkswagen campaign used public mistrust with Madison Avenue hard sell as the basis for convincing sales arguments.

By the nineties it was common for ads to draw attention to their conventions. In the UK, the 'No Nonsense' campaign for John Smith's Bitter featured Jack Dee complaining about the gimmicks he was forced to endure by the makers of the ads.

Around the same time, Sprite launched its 'Image is nothing. Thirst is everything' campaign, parodying ad clichés. In one execution, the cast of a patronizing urban soft drink ad set in a basketball court are revealed to be vain, plummy actors. In another, a family react to a mascot leaping off a drink carton with understandable terror.

Although less popular now, this kind of self-awareness still crops up when there are new clichés to expose. In an ad for Tango Clear, an office worker is drenched with water after sipping the drink. When her boss questions her, she explains that it's a visual metaphor.

A more serious variation of self-awareness occurs when a brand crusades against dishonest advertising conventions. Dove's Real Beauty campaign exposes the unattainable images at the dark heart of fashion advertising.

01 / Dove
This viral clip for Dove exposed how image manipulation creates unrealistic depictions of beauty in fashion advertising.

02 / VW
'We finally came up with a beautiful picture of a Volkswagen'. Volkswagen ads in the sixties subverted reader expectation.

03 / Sprite
When a mascot springs to life in this self-aware Sprite commercial, the family are understandably horrified.

01

03

We finally came up with a beautiful picture of a Volkswagen.

A Volkswagen starts looking good when everything else starts looking bad.

Let's say it's late at night and you can't sleep. It's 10 below and you forgot to put antifreeze in your car.

(A Volkswagen doesn't use antifreeze. Its engine is cooled by air.)

Let's say it's now morning: You start your car and the gas gauge reads Empty.

(Even with a gallon left, you should go approximately 27 miles in a VW.)

Let's say you notice on your way out of the driveway that every other car on your block is stuck in the snow.

(A VW goes very well in snow because the engine is in the back. It gives the rear wheels much better traction.)

Let's say you make it into town and the only parking space is half a space between a snow plow and a big, fat wall.

(A VW is small enough to fit into half a parking space.)

Let's say it's now 9:15 a.m. and the only other guy in the office is your boss.

(Now what could be more beautiful than that?)

02

*Anti-advertising appears
to criticize the product
to reach resistant audiences.*

39

ANTI-ADVERTISING

01 / Hans Brinker
When the Hans Brinker Budget Hotel boasts about its poor facilities, it's actually drawing attention to its low prices.

02 / Goebel Beer
This vintage Goebel Beer ad used self-criticism for an aggressive product relaunch. An interesting but risky strategy.

03 / Pot Noodle
'That felt so wrong and yet it felt so right'. Pot Noodle is a shameful pleasure in this self-deprecating campaign.

Going further than self-awareness, the anti-ad subverts conventions further by denigrating the product.

In his celebrated rant against advertising, the stand-up comedian Bill Hicks imagines industry types approving of him for going after the 'anti-marketing dollar'. In fact, this sort of Orwellian double-think does go on. Some campaigns have adopted a self-critical viewpoint to reach resistant audiences.

In 2002, the soft drink Tango Tropical launched with the line 'Don't slag it off until you've tried it. (*Then slag it off.*)' This tone uses self-criticism to pre-empt the hostile reaction of jaded consumers.

Some campaigns celebrate the shortcomings of their product. Few would class the dehydrated UK snack Pot Noodle as quality cuisine, but not everyone wants their snacks to be classy.

In the 'Slag of all Snacks' campaign, a man leaves his wife behind to visit a red-light district and buy a 'filthy' Pot Noodle.

Many apparent anti-ads actually highlight an important proposition. A campaign for Amsterdam's Hans Brinker Budget Hotel boasts about losing luggage, ignoring complaints, disturbing customers in the morning and running out of toilet paper. The real message is that the hotel is the place to book if price is your only consideration.

These approaches might seem risky or counter-intuitive, but they can work for the right product. As Bill Hicks might recognize, ironic, knowing consumerism is still consumerism.

HANS BRINKER BUDGET HOTEL. IT CAN'T GET ANY WORSE.

BUT WE'LL DO OUR BEST.
AMSTERDAM +31 20 6220687

01

One of the best
things about
new Goebel Beer
is that it doesn't taste
anything like
old Goebel Beer.

02

03

40

ADVERTISING PARODIES

Lots of ads spoof other ads, campaigns and genres. Parody can be a smart way of hijacking the popularity of a rival campaign and standing out.

Some spoofs apply a famous endline to a different brand. In the eighties, Club biscuits ran a campaign with the line 'If you like a lot of chocolate on your biscuit, join our club'. The Leith Agency ran the same line for local gym the Edinburgh Club.

Famous ads with a straight tone are often subject to mundane or silly remakes, as in the Tango spoof of Sony Bravia 'Balls' and the 118 118 send-up of Honda 'Cog'. The danger of these in-jokes is that they can be more popular with the advertising industry than with the public.

Some ads send up styles that have become clichéd, such as testimonials, product demos and doorstep challenges. These parodies are most satisfying when they identify a new trend, such as 'Big Ad' for Australian lager Carlton Draught, which spoofed event ads that rely solely on scale and budget.

One of the dangers of spoofing is that parodies of clichés can become clichés in their own right. The serious tone of charity ads has now been sent up so much the surprise has gone. But there can still be fresh twists, such as the 'Feet' spot for Fox Sports, which shows a man changing a baby's nappy with his feet. A pull-back reveal shows that he isn't disabled, but addicted to the Fox Sports website.

01

02

03

41

Creating a brand character is an efficient way to deliver a variety of messages.

BRAND MASCOTS

01

In *The Simpsons* episode 'Attack of the 50ft Eyesores', hundreds of advertising mascots come to life and terrorize Springfield. It's a great commentary on the subliminal power of brand mascots. Like Hitchcock's birds, they surround us, and are more powerful than we assume.

The mascot is one of the most popular advertising devices of all; a mascot can transcend its timeslot and become a global pop culture icon on a par with characters from movies and TV shows.

Mascots can also help with difficult creative briefs. If a brand wants to communicate a lot of different propositions, it can be hard to produce a single-minded idea. But a brand mascot can bring together a wide variety of messages in a visually consistent campaign.

Some memorable mascots have been generated by wordplay on a brand name, such as the Geico gecko and the Comparethemarket.com meerkat. Some, like the Duracell and Energizer bunnies, began as product demonstrations. Others have their roots in borrowed interest, such as Ronald McDonald, a variation on clown characters that were popular on television in the early sixties, such as Bozo the Clown.

Popular icons can survive for decades, sometimes even outliving their brands. A knitted monkey character created for the short-lived UK satellite service ITV Digital was so popular it was revived for PG Tips tea.

01 / Duracell Bunny
Sometimes a product demonstration can create a brand mascot. In the case of Duracell, it was a battery-powered toy rabbit.

02 / PG Tips
Mascots can outlive the brand they're made for. This monkey puppet, created for ITV Digital, was inherited by tea brand PG Tips.

03 / Compare the Market
Aleksandr Orlov is a meerkat created for price comparison site Comparethemarket.com. In initial executions, the character was annoyed that everyone was confusing the site with his own, Comparethemeerkat.com.

Sometimes the product itself can be turned into a brand mascot.

42

BRINGING THE PRODUCT TO LIFE

01 / Starkist Tuna
Charlie the Tuna was created for Starkist Tuna by Leo Burnett in the early sixties. This hip cartoon tuna wanted to be tinned and eaten.

02 / Pillsbury
Poppin' Fresh was a brand character created from dough to promote a range of baking products.

03 / Peperami
'It's a bit of an animal'. This anarchic character finds himself so tasty he eats his own arms.

Sticking arms and legs on a product might not seem like a great creative leap, but this technique has created popular and enduring campaigns.

Many of the most famous advertising icons of the twentieth century were anthropomorphic figures, including Mr. Peanut for Planter's Peanuts, StarKist tuna's Charlie the Tuna, the M&M characters, the Kool-Aid Man and Poppin' Fresh, more commonly known as the Pillsbury Doughboy.

These characters often became so popular they inspired spin-off merchandising. Singing raisins from a California Raisin Marketing Board campaign featured on four spin-off records, an animated TV series and a Nintendo game.

Not all brand characters need to be loveable, though. An eighties campaign for UK breakfast cereal Weetabix depicted the product as a skinhead gang, complete with an aggressive Bob Hoskins voiceover and the endline 'If you know what's good for you'. These characters were also popular enough for a game adaptation, this time a *Space Invaders* knock-off for early home computers such as the Sinclair ZX Spectrum.

An even less sympathetic character was devised for meat snack Peperami, which featured an aggressive, self-cannibalizing creature voiced by comedian Ade Edmunson. The endline was, 'It's a bit of an animal'.

01

02

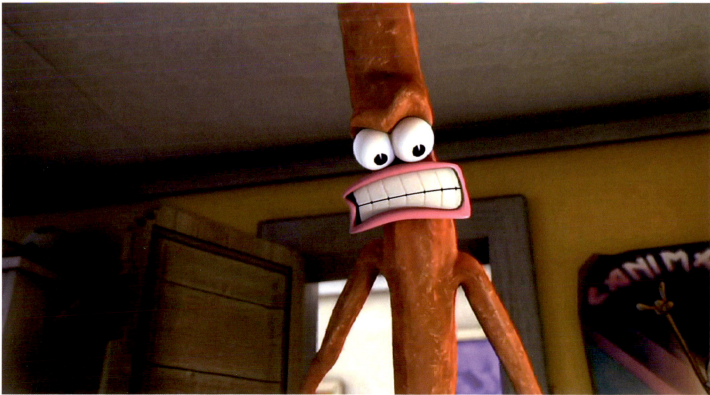

03

43

PERSONIFICATION

01/ Nestea
This Nestea ad personifies the product as a revenge-seeking action hero. It makes for a fresh take on a very familiar proposition.

02/ Apple
'I'm a Mac … And I'm a PC'. Personification can be an efficient way of covering a wide range of messages.

03/ Guinness
Not all brand personifications are positive. This pint of Guinness is selfish and unsympathetic, a play on the double meaning of the word 'cold'.

You don't have to attach arms and legs to a product to make it seem human. Personification compares brands to people in much subtler ways.

Lots of famous endlines employ personification, from 'Like a good neighbour, State Farm is there' to 'Milk's gotta lotta bottle'.

Headlines can develop comparisons between brands and people, as with CDP's Martell brandy ad, 'Sip it with respect. It's probably older than you are.'

A less reverent campaign for Guinness Extra Cold featured the pint saying things like 'Because she's younger and better looking than you', and 'Can we go back to your place? I'd rather you didn't know where I live.'

Performers and celebrities are often used to stand for brands on radio and TV. A famous example is Apple's 'Get a Mac' campaign, in which a hipster played by Justin Long represents a Mac, and a stuffy character played by John Hodgman represents a PC. This approach allowed Apple to make direct comparisons with competing brands, covering a wide range of product messages in one consistent and successful campaign.

01

02

03

44

CATCHPHRASES

Some ads feature words or phrases that pass into widespread use. This can happen by accident or because of a deliberate attempt to write something that catches on.

Brands can create a catchphrase by repeating the same thing over and over again in a single execution. Budweiser's classic 'Whassup' ad managed to repeat the phrase over ten times in the space of 60 seconds. The ad was adapted from a short film by director Charles Stone III, who also stars in it. It's the sort of ad that would be very difficult to sell to a client on the basis of a script alone, as all the humour comes from the performance.

A 1984 commercial for the Wendy's fast-food chain featured 81-year-old actress Clara Peller shouting 'Where's the beef?' three times. The repetition helped the phrase pass into popular culture, and it was mimicked hundreds of times on TV, radio and in films. The phrase even entered political discourse when it was used by Democratic candidate Walter Mondale as part of his election campaign.

Sometimes, unintentional catchphrases are created simply by brands sticking with the same execution for a long time. An ad for Ferrero Rocher that ran in the UK throughout the nineties showed an 'ambassador's reception' in which guests were served chocolates from silver trays. One of the women says, 'Monsieur, with these Rocher you're really spoiling us.' The line has been parodied hundreds of times since in shows such as *Father Ted* and *Little Britain*.

01 / Wendy's
'Where's the beef?' This famous question was repeated three times in a 30-second ad, spawning a catchphrase that survives to this day.

02 / Budweiser
'Whasssssuuuuuuuup ppppp?' This classic catchphrase was referenced in *Scary Movie*, *The Simpsons*, Adam Sandler movies and in a million bar conversations.

03 / Ferrero Rocher
'Monsieur, with these Rocher you're really spoiling us.' An unintentional catchphrase was spawned by this long-running ad for Ferrero Rocher.

01

03

02

45

Some campaigns are based around invented words, which are often inspired by brand names.

NEOLOGISMS

Advertising agencies and branding consultancies often coin new words when they're naming a new brand or sub-brand, but words can be created for ad campaigns too.

Many brand names enter common speech, sometimes transforming from noun to verb, as with the example of 'Hoover'. Many endlines try and contrive this, as with 'You know when you've been Tango'd'.

Some brand names become 'generic trademarks' and stand for their entire class of product, such as Biro, Frisbee, iPod, Post-it, Sellotape and Velcro. A big advertising push can sometimes make a brand name seem synonymous with a sector, making everything else seem like an imitation.

Neologisms created for advertising campaigns are often bits of wordplay centred around a brand name. When regulations meant that the popular but scientifically questionable endline 'Guinness is good for you' couldn't run anymore, it was inverted to 'Guinnless isn't good for you'. The campaign included a self-help group called 'Friends of the Guinnless' in sympathy for those who had to go without the stout.

The breakfast cereal Weetabix ran a similar campaign based around two invented words, 'Withabix' and 'Withoutabix'. It consisted of entertaining visual hyperboles of success and failure.

A classic US ad for the artificial leather brand Naugahyde created a fictional creature called the 'Nauga', which produced the material by shedding its skin. Nauga dolls became a popular merchandising spin-off and can still be bought today.

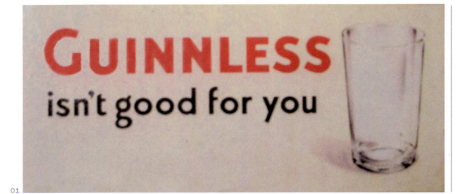

01

02

03

01 / Guinness
This neat reversal of 'Guinness is good for you' coined the word 'Guinnless'. Neologisms are often based around brand names.

02 / Weetabix
This British campaign for breakfast cereal Weetabix was centred around two neologisms, 'Withabix' and 'Withoutabix'.

03 / Naugahyde
The ad for artificial leather Naugahyde invented a new word, a brand mascot and a piece of merchandise that still sells today.

46

LONG COPY

It's often claimed that no one reads body copy anymore. Indeed, copy has largely gone missing from press ads over the last couple of decades, so they probably don't even get a chance to. Is the long copy really an outmoded format?

A simple answer could be that anything unusual in advertising is worth trying because it will stand out. As the old maxim goes, 'If you can't be good be different'. It's also worth remembering that you aren't necessarily meant to read long-copy ads all the way through.

Sometimes large blocks of text can bestow a feeling of quality on a product, whether you read them or not. Chunks of copy can also be used to imply the scale of a problem. An ad for Breast Cancer awareness by Saatchi & Saatchi Malaysia ran six columns of dense text under the line 'You might get breast cancer if …'. Another execution featured dense copy under the line 'How to remove a breast', and just a few lines about self-examination under the line 'How to save a breast'.

Another reason to use long copy might be to deliberately evoke an old-fashioned style of advertising. This might be to emphasize the heritage of a brand, or because a campaign is themed around nostalgia. In the UK, the eighties chocolate bar Wispa was revived with eighties-style long-copy ads.

Finally, even if you don't believe modern audiences will plough through thousands of words of body copy, it's worth considering ads with long headlines, such as the Tide example here. Consumers can surely find time in their busy schedules to read 100 words if they're well-written enough.

WHEN THE KETCHUP I WAS COACHING WON THE LITTLE LEAGUE WORLD KETCHUP, I WAS PRETTY STOKED. I DIDN'T THINK WE COULD PULL IT OFF. IT WAS THE BOTTOM OF THE SIXTH KETCHUP AND WE WERE DOWN BY THREE KETCHUPS. EDDIE MARKUM WAS UP TO THE KETCHUP FIRST KETCHUP. IT'S A SWING AND A KETCHUP. NEXT KETCHUP. MORE OF THE GAME. LAST KETCHUP. EDDIE KNOCKS IT OUT OF THE KETCHUP. SEE YA! THE GERBILS WIN THE WORLD KETCHUP! THE GERBILS WIN THE KETCHUP.

REMEMBER THE DAY. NOT THE STAIN. **Tide**

Full Page Yo, baby! Stand waaay back. I am a *full page ad*. Printers are scared of me - they call me the 'great white'. There ain't no ad like me. You want hard sell? I'll give you hard sell. I'll sell your whole shop. I'll carry ten washing machines, ten tumble driers, fifty cameras and then ask, "Hey, what about those widescreen TVs you wanna shift?" But I'm more than all that. You launching a product? I'll launch your product - I'll launch it into space. You got a picture? Blow it up, I ain't afraid. You got words? Bring 'em on. Big or small, when they're on me, they look important. Because I *announce*. I got the *dimensions*. I am the undisputed heavyweight king of press advertising and I will make your product my queen. Hear me roar. **The Power of Press**

02

01

YOU RISK GETTING BREAST CANCER IF:

03

47

THE CURIOSITY AROUSER

01 / Albany Life Assurance
Insurance ads aren't known for being exciting, but this vintage Albany Life ad attracted readers with a macabre promise.

02 / Timberland
Good storytelling can arouse curiosity. This long-copy campaign for Timberland found compelling ways to describe long-lasting outdoor wear.

03 / Honda
This Honda spot starring Matthew Broderick was trailed by a classic 'teaser'.

The technique of arousing reader curiosity was popular in the days of long-copy ads. Albany Life Assurance ran a questionnaire ad with the headline 'Answer these ten questions and work out the date of your own death'. An ad for Timberland drew readers into a story with the line 'Your eyes are frozen. Your skin has turned black. You're technically dead. Let's talk boots.'

A more recent ad for McDonald's enticed readers by weighing in on a topical debate. Morgan Spurlock's film *Super Size Me*, which was highly critical of the chain, had generated a lot of comment about fast food. Anyone who'd been following the discussion would have wanted to know the company's official response.

Another type of curiosity arouser is the 'teaser ad', which gives a small, cryptic taste of a coming campaign or product launch. Honda trailed their 2012 Super Bowl ad with a ten-second spot showing Matthew Broderick drawing curtains aside and saying, 'How can I handle work on a day like today?' The clip generated online speculation that Broderick was about to announce a sequel to *Ferris Bueller's Day Off*. It was actually a teaser for a Bueller-themed ad.

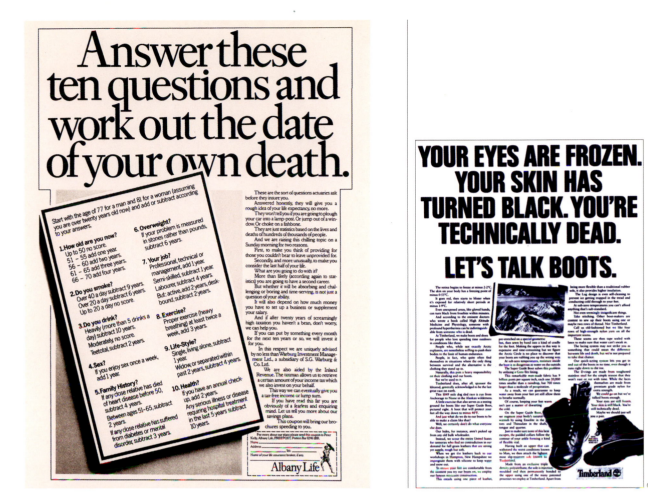

48

ARGUMENTS

Some ads manage to condense convincing arguments into just a few words.

Traditional ad copy is based around the sales argument, a procession of logical points leading to the conclusion that the product should be bought. It's a tradition that continues today, though often in condensed form.

A vintage IBM ad made the case that technology is a promise rather than a threat in a reasoned long-copy argument. The notion that computer technology is something to be wary of is made to seem absurd through comparisons with fears about the steam engine. The copy puts contemporary discomfort about computer technology into a wider context, arguing that it's 'given man time to create, and released him from the day-to-day tasks that limit his self-fulfilment'.

In a similar twist of logic to the reverse testimonial, copy can include points that seem to contradict its argument but are actually trivial. An ad for *The Economist* listed the magazine's pros as 'Sparkling conversation, improved career prospects, extreme wealth, ennoblement and immortality'. There was a cons column next to it, but all it said was, 'Slight risk of paper cuts'.

Great headlines can condense an argument into a single line. A gun-control ad making the case that .22 handguns should be banned too showed a picture of Robert Kennedy. The headline was, 'If a .22 handgun is less deadly, why isn't he less dead?'

Two men were watching a mechanical excavator on a building site.

There are two ways to regard technological development. As a threat. Or as a promise. Every invention from the wheel to the steam engine created the same dilemma.

"If it wasn't for that machine," said one,

But it's only by exploiting the promise of each that man has managed to improve his lot.

Computer technology has given man more time to create, and released him from the day-to-day tasks that limit his self fulfilment.

"twelve men with shovels could be doing that job."

We ourselves are very heavy users of this technology ranging from golf ball typewriters to ink-jet printers to small and large computers, so we're more aware than most of that age-old dilemma threat or promise.

"Yes," replied the other, "and if it wasn't for your twelve shovels, two hundred men with teaspoons could be doing that job."

Yet during 27 years in the UK our work-force has increased from six to 15,000. And during those 27 years not a single person has been laid off, not a single day has been lost through strikes.

Throughout Britain, electronic technology has shortened queues. Streamlined efficiency. Boosted exports.

And kept British products competitive in an international market.

To treat technology as a threat would halt progress. As a promise it makes tomorrow look a lot brighter.

IBM

IBM United Kingdom Limited P.O. Box 41. North Harbour Portsmouth Hampshire PO6 3AU

01

01 / IBM
Long-copy ads can argue their cases one reasoned point at a time. This vintage IBM ad makes the case that technology is progress rather than threat.

02 / Handgun
This gun-control ad featuring Robert Kennedy makes the case for banning .22 handguns in just 12 words.

03 / The Economist
Just like salesmen, ads can throw out trivial cases against their argument to make it look as though they're considering both sides.

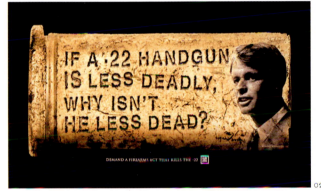

IF A .22 HANDGUN IS LESS DEADLY, WHY ISN'T HE LESS DEAD?

DEMAND A FIREARMS ACT THAT KILLS THE .22

02

Pros:

Sparkling conversation
Improved career prospects
Extreme wealth
Ennoblement
Immortality

Cons:

Slight risk of paper cuts

The Economist

03

49

Starting with a few words of friendly advice is a classic technique of the salesman. It's a method that many ads have adopted.

ADVICE

01/ Plymouth Gin
'Plymouth Gin is not the only way to tell a gentleman'. Some campaigns offer advice on lateral subjects to help with brand positioning.

02/ Tampax
This tampon ad adopted the kind of friendly tone often found in teen magazine advice columns.

Some products suit the empathetic tone of the magazine advice column. AMV's print ads for Tampax in the nineties did a great job of evoking the embarrassment of puberty and then introducing the product. It made for a warm and understanding tone that was more effective than the patronizing lifestyle imagery used by much rival advertising.

Advice can sometimes be offered on more lateral topics to help position a brand. A campaign for Plymouth Gin gave advice on subjects such as 'The selection and maintenance of a stout pair of shoes'. The endline was, 'Plymouth Gin is not the only way to tell a gentleman'. This approach to press advertising was a kind of precursor to the 'branded content' approach that's become popular in recent years.

Lots of ads have offered tongue-in-cheek advice, often in the style of books such as *The Worst-Case Scenario Survival Handbook*. An ad for the Ragged Mountain Resort in New Hampshire advised, 'Always remember to introduce yourself to the person next to you in the lift line. It's always good to have someone else around who can identify your body.'

THE SELECTION AND MAINTENANCE OF A STOUT PAIR OF SHOES.

CHOOSING THE SHOE.

Shoes may be divided into two principal categories: A. Those that are worn by gentlemen. B. Other shoes.

A shoe may only be said to belong to the former category once it meets three main criteria. (i) That it is hand stitched on a last specially made for the customer. (ii) That the very finest hides are employed in its construction (Russian Calf, Grain Hide, Doe-Skin and Antelope are entirely adequate.) (iii) That its design (usually following the Oxford or Derby pattern) makes absolutely no concessions whatsoever to the fashions of the day.

Footwear that is mass-produced from *imitation leather,* or that employs *composition soles,* or that is conceived in *modish designs and colours* does not merit our further attention.

A CAVEAT REGARDING HEEL-HEIGHT.

The prescribed height for the shoe heel is 1¼". Any shoe that attempts, via the artifice of a built-up heel, to increase the apparent height of its owner, will merely succeed in *reducing his stature as a gentleman.*

THE CORRECT METHOD OF LACING.

It is of paramount importance that the laces of a good shoe be threaded in exact accordance with the scheme illustrated opposite. This is known as the McPherson's Loop.

By threading the off-side bee directly through to the near-side rear hole, an equal pressure is thereby exerted across the shoe's upper when the laces are pulled tight.

It should be borne in mind that external criss-cross lacing is a practice normally confined to the *sporting plimsoll;* if found on any other shoe, it is fairly certain that such footwear falls into category B. previously referred to.

CLEANING THE SHOE.

As in 1. remove all traces of peat bog, sphagnum moss etc. with a good quality damp rag. If the shoe is very wet, then air it naturally in a warm place (never in front of a fire). When barely damp, insert the tree.

2. Apply sparingly a coat of finest grade wax polish, using a special curry brush to ensure complete penetration into the *welt-recesses.* Although older shoes will need more polish, never apply in excess as this often *clogs the broguing.*

3. Wait approximately ten minutes whilst the wax is thoroughly absorbed into the leather. Then polish briskly with a brush made from the very best goat hair.

4. Finally, finish off with a freshly-laundered duster to attain maximum brilliance.

N.B. On no account submit any shoe to the indignity of the *automatic electric polisher.* These machines, often to be found lurking at railway termini and in lesser hotels, are notorious for their complete lack of discrimination as to the hue of polish applied. Furthermore, they have been known on occasion to impart a *deep-gloss lustre* to a *gentleman's turn-up.*

THE IMPORTANCE OF THE TREE.

The consistent use of a proper shoe tree is amongst the foremost desiderata for correct shoe maintenance. Trees of the best pedigree are hand-fashioned by the original last maker from either Mahogany or seasoned Beech. They invariably conform to the three-piece wedged design as illustrated in 'A'.

At all costs do not insert into a good shoe any implement that bears even a passing resemblance to 'B'. This may cause lasting damage to the shoe's shape, not to mention *the owner's prospects for social advancement.*

THE CORRECT PREPARATION OF A GIN AND TONIC.

Unless a bottle of Plymouth Gin is plainly in evidence at the drinks table, all further efforts to create the definitive gin and tonic should be abandoned forthwith.

As is generally accepted by those knowledgeable in such matters, Plymouth stands alone in possessing the requisite *dryness* and *vigour of nose* for this most refreshing of libations.

(This is due in no small part to the inordinate length of *drying time* lavished upon the juniper berries and sundry botanicals employed in its manufacture.)

Plymouth should always be served in a large 8oz lead crystal tumbler, with a proprietary brand of tonic, thinly-sliced lemon or lime and generous quantities of freshly broken ice.

It should also be noted that the suggestion *'ice and a slice, squire?'* is a fairly reliable indicator that the gin you are being offered is not Plymouth, but another distillation of somewhat dubious provenance.

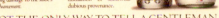

PLYMOUTH GIN IS NOT THE ONLY WAY TO TELL A GENTLEMAN.

01

Ads sometimes insult readers to generate humour or shock.

50

INSULTS

Although it's much rarer, an ad can be based around an insult as well as a compliment. It can be a shock tactic to help a charity or public service message cut through, or it can be an ironic tone adopted for a knowing, marketing-savvy audience.

Saatchi & Saatchi's ad for Anti-Slavery International had the headline 'Read this you piece of shit'. The copy explains, 'If you're offended by this advert, you should be. Nobody should be treated like this. Yet unfortunately, there are millions of people around the world who are.'

A campaign for Friends of Animals insulted fur wearers with the endline 'Fur is a thing of the past. Evolve.' Executions included 'Fur wearers: Please refrain from eating the squirrels' and ' Fur wearers: Please refrain from climbing traffic lights, marking territory and/or sniffing other pedestrian's crotches.'

Satirical newspaper and website *The Onion* adopted an insulting tone of voice for a marketing campaign in 2005, and their fans would probably have been disappointed by anything less. Headlines included '3 out 4 readers shouldn't' and 'Subscribing says a lot about you and your need for psychotherapy'. Meanwhile, its entertainment spin-off, the AV Club, adopted the endline 'Helping nerds become snobs'.

PLEASE SEND COMMENTS OR COMPLAINTS TO:

**YOUR ASS
1019 YOURASS AVE.
YOURASS, YA 10012**

the ONION

01

01 / **The Onion**
The world's leading satire brand adopts an insulting tone of voice for their marketing, just as fans would want.

02 / **Anti-Slavery**
'Read this you piece of shit'. It's a headline that's almost impossible to ignore, but fortunately the subject matter justifies the approach.

03 / **Friends of Animals**
This campaign for Friends of Animals was a series of insults directed at fur wearers. Confrontational language is often used to challenge attitudes.

READ THIS YOU PIECE OF SHIT.

If you're offended by this advertisement, you should be.

Nobody should be treated like this.

Yet unfortunately, there are millions of people around the world who are.

For many, a verbal lashing is the very least they have to worry about.

In Brazil, for example, Amazonian estate workers face a punishment called 'the trunk'.

A man who hasn't felled his quota of trees, is stripped, tied up and left in a hollowed out tree-trunk for three days.

As if that isn't punishment enough, the trunk is first smeared with honey to attract ants and other insects.

In India, children face similar horrors. Kids as young as six are sold to work in carpet factories.

When the loom-masters can't find enough children to buy, they kidnap them.

The kids are made to work all day. If they slow down at all, they are not allowed to sleep at night. If they make a mistake, they are beaten.

One child was doused with paraffin and set ablaze because he asked for time off. Six others were so viciously beaten for just playing, one of them died.

In Nepal, slavery is just as widespread. Ten year old girls are abducted and sold into prostitution in India.

First, they have to go through a 'grooming' period. Stripped naked, they are locked in a tiny room for days at a time without food.

They are burnt with cigarettes, beaten and raped until eventually they become totally submissive. Only then will they fetch the highest prices from Bombay's brothel keepers.

Just as prostitution can be a form of slavery, so can marriage.

In many parts of the world parents still control who their daughters wed. Who they choose very much depends on what the groom's family offers in exchange. The bride's welfare matters little.

Consequently, there are many women forced to marry against their will. Some even as young as nine. One twelve year old Nigerian girl hated her husband so much, she kept trying to run away from him.

To stop her, he hacked off both her legs. As you can see, slavery isn't a thing of the past.

Nor is it just a problem of the Third World.

In Britain alone, there have been 1700 cases of abused domestic servants reported since 1987. Most of them are young girls from poor backgrounds overseas. They see working in Britain as an answer to their problems.

But when they get here, they are often treated no better than animals. Many are made to sleep on the floor and just fed scraps. They have to work an 18 hour day. If they complain, they're beaten or caned. Some aren't even allowed out. Some are raped.

The list of atrocities goes on and on.

There are still over 100 million slaves in the world. Each one probably has a story as pain-filled as these.

Anti Slavery International campaigns for the abolition of slavery. We know that it's only by making the facts of these people's lives known and by bringing slavery out into the open that we'll ever destroy it.

Indeed, by lobbying and by raising world awareness of these issues, we've persuaded governments and the UN to tackle the problem.

In some countries like Thailand, India and Pakistan we've even pushed them into changing the law.

None of this would have been possible without the help of our supporters. They have sent letters and asked questions of individuals, companies and governments all around the world.

To keep the pressure on them, we need your help in our forthcoming campaigns.

If you'd like to be involved, fill out the coupon below and become a member. In time, we'll make sure no one knows what it feels like to be treated as a slave.

ANTI-SLAVERY INTERNATIONAL

Anti-Slavery International, Stableyard, Broomgrove Rd, London SW9 9TL. Tel: 0171-924 9555. Fax: 0171-738 4110.

I would like to join ASI: £15 Individual membership ☐ £5 Student, Unwaged ☐ I would/would not like more information. Name _____
Address _____ Postcode _____ I would like to donate £ _____ Payment can be made by cheque or postal order (payable to Anti-Slavery International) or by credit card. Mastercard ☐ Visa ☐ Amex ☐ Diners ☐ Number ☐☐☐☐☐☐☐☐☐☐☐☐☐☐☐ Expires ☐☐☐☐

FUR WEARERS:

PLEASE REFRAIN FROM CLIMBING TRAFFIC LIGHTS, MARKING TERRITORY AND/OR SNIFFING OTHER PEDESTRIAN'S CROTCHES.

–BUREAU OF SANITATION

FUR IS A THING OF THE PAST. EVOLVE.
Friends of Animals

03

51

Flattering the target audience can be effective if you get the tone right.

COMPLIMENTS

01 / Chivas Regal
A list of compliments written to a father, this Chivas Regal ad is a great example of long copy.

02 / Nike
'Most heroes are anonymous'. Nike have a history of paying compliments to their sporty audience in a credible way.

03 / The Economist
The Economist's 'White out of red' campaign complimented its audience with consistent wit and intelligence.

As anyone who's ever been hassled by a clothes shop assistant telling them how great they'd look in an expensive pair of jeans knows, flattering the customer is a common sales technique.

From L'Oréal telling us we're 'worth it' to private healthcare firm Bupa telling us we're 'amazing', many ad lines are written as compliments. It's a difficult tone to get right, as laying on the flattery too thick can come across as desperate.

Sports brands such as Nike and Adidas often get the tone just right. A Nike press ad showed a shaft of light picking out a runner in a city with the line 'Most heroes are anonymous'. It evoked the small moments of triumph in the life of the amateur athlete in a convincing way.

The 'White out of red' campaign for *The Economist* set the standard for complimenting the intelligence of an audience in a witty way. One execution read, 'A poster should contain no more than eight words, which is the maximum the average reader can take in at a single glance. This, however, is a poster for Economist readers.'

Compliments can inspire gift-buying, as in David Abbott's classic long-copy ad for Chivas Regal. It explains what a Father's Day gift of the whisky really means, in a warm tone that never quite lapses into sentimentality.

Because I've known you all my life.

Because a red Rudge bicycle once made me the happiest boy on the street.

Because you let me play cricket on the lawn.

Because you used to dance in the kitchen with a tea-towel round your waist.

Because your cheque book was always busy on my behalf.

Because our house was always full of books and laughter.

Because of countless Saturday mornings you gave up to watch a small boy play rugby.

Because you never expected too much of me or let me get away with too little.

Because of all the nights you sat working at your desk while I lay sleeping in my bed.

Because you never embarrassed me by talking about the birds and the bees.

Because I know there's a faded newspaper clipping in your wallet about my scholarship.

Because you always made me polish the heels of my shoes as brightly as the toes.

Because you've remembered my birthday 38 times out of 38.

Because you still hug me when we meet.

Because you still buy my mother flowers.

Because you've more than your fair share of grey hairs and I know who helped put them there.

Because you're a marvellous grandfather.

Because you made my wife feel one of the family.

Because you wanted to go to McDonalds the last time I bought you lunch.

Because you've always been there when I've needed you.

Because you let me make my own mistakes and never once said "I told you so."

Because you still pretend you only need glasses for reading.

Because I don't say thank you as often as I should.

Because it's Father's Day.

Because if you don't deserve Chivas Regal, who does?

01

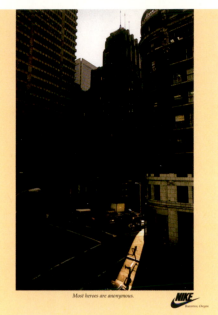

Most heroes are anonymous.

NIKE
Beaverton, Oregon

02

"Can I phone an Economist reader please Chris?"

03

52

*Setting a challenge can be
a good way to engage readers
and viewers.*

CHALLENGES

01

Writing a headline or endline in the form of a challenge or dare can help an ad cut through.

A Western Union ad from the early sixties showed a picture of a telegram under the headline 'Ignore it'. Rather than just claiming that telegrams are hard to ignore, the ad proved it.

Several classic campaigns of the sixties, seventies and eighties were written as challenges. In the US, Lays were betting everyone they couldn't eat just one potato chip. In the UK, Shredded Wheat bet customers they couldn't eat three, and Fruit Pastels bet they couldn't put one in their mouth without chewing it. Today's audience might be slightly more wary of such blatant attempts to make them consume more, however.

Challenges are often used in recruitment campaigns for teachers, nurses, the police and the army. A London police recruitment ad showed a man spitting at a police officer with the line 'Could you turn the other cheek?' Recruitment campaigns that stress the difficulty of a profession can attract the right applicants and also make existing staff feel better about what they do.

Many online campaigns are based around challenges. Crispin Porter and Bogusky's 'Whopper Sacrifice' campaign for Burger King offered customers a free Whopper if they deleted ten Facebook friends. It was a challenge that many rose to, and over 200, 000 people were unfriended before Burger King suspended the campaign.

01 / Western Union

You can't ignore a telegram. This Western Union ad proves its point by writing the headline in the form of a challenge.

02 / Burger King

The true value of friendship. Burger King challenged Facebook users to delete ten friends in exchange for a Whopper, and thousands did.

03 / Shredded Wheat

Challenges relating to product consumption were once common. Even Jaws from the James Bond franchise couldn't eat three in a TV execution of this campaign.

02

Bet you can't eat three.

Shredded Wheat. 100% whole wheat.

03

53

CRUSADES

01 / Million
A genuine social crusade. These phones were given out free to New York school children, and credit was awarded for good attendance and grades.

02 / Small Business Saturday
The 'Small Business Saturday' campaign from American Express encouraged customers to support independent local shops.

03 / Pedigree
Crusades can work well if they're credible for a brand. Pedigree launched an adoption drive as part of its 'We're for dogs' campaign.

Many campaigns use the language of social crusades. This can be either a playful adoption of tone or a genuine attempt to address a social problem.

Many campaigns depict people holding banners and staging rallies on behalf of a brand. In the UK, Ikea's 'Chuck out your chintz' campaign showed people on a suburban street throwing out old-fashioned home furnishings in favour of the minimal styles of the Swedish retailer. It was a shift in interior design tastes dressed up as revolution.

Rather than simply using the language of crusades, some campaigns genuinely attempt to address issues. Droga5's 'Million' campaign for the New York Department of Education and TracFone Wireless gave free 'incentive-based' phones to school students. Credit on the phones was awarded for improved attendance and grades, and 75 per cent of parents reported that their children were studying harder as a result of the scheme.

Crispin Porter and Bogusky's 'Small Business Saturday' campaign for American Express was a crusade on behalf of independent stores. It encouraged customers to avoid chains and visit small local shops on the day after Black Friday. It was estimated that over 100 million people shopped small on the day, including President Barack Obama.

01

02

03

54

References that make sense only to certain social groups are common in social and online interaction. Advertising can use in-jokes, although making them work well can require research.

IN-JOKES

Unlike millions of other websites, we know exactly what you are looking for. Find expert analysis of global business at **ft.com**

We live in **FINANCIAL TIMES**®

enterprise modelling | Search

01

Unsurprisingly, the in-jokes that creative departments pull off most successfully are those for the advertising industry itself. After a round of redundancies had shaken London agencies, an ad for an advertising five-a-side football competition ran with the headline 'Good news. You only need five players.' In the US, copywriter Tom McElligott had such a reputation for dominating creative awards that his retirement was referenced in a call-for-entries ad.

A campaign for the *Financial Times* featured literal interpretations of business jargon such as 'enterprise modelling', 'baby bond', 'record fall' and 'third-quarter stats'. It was an entertaining way to prove that the paper spoke the language of its target audience.

In-jokes can also be used effectively in recruitment advertising. Design agency This is Real Art ran an ad for a web developer that was written entirely in code. It made the ad cut through to people who were qualified for the position, and it also looked suitably unusual and stylish.

Sadly, not all business-to-business and recruitment advertising manages to use in-jokes this well. Creatives in these sectors seem happy to settle for puns and visual metaphors instead of uncovering the shared references that will engage their target audiences.

```php
<?php
class WebDeveloper extends ThisisRealArt {

    const constant   = 'opportunities';

    public  $company = 'This is Real Art';
    public  $address = '2 Sycamore St, London, EC1Y 0SF';
    public  $phone   = '020 7253 2181';
    private $email   = 'info@thisisrealart.com';

    public function getRecruit(){

        // What do we require?
        $this->db->select('webDeveloper');

        // From where are we selecting?
        $this->db->from('peopleWhoLoveIdeas');

        // Select criteria
        $where = "'PHP OOP & mySQL'  = 'strong'
                AND 'XHTML & CSS'   = 'strict'
                AND ('jQuery'       = 'bonus'
                    OR 'linux'      = 'bonus'
                    OR 'flash'      = 'bonus') ";
        $this->db->where($where);

        // How should we prioritize?
        $orderBy = array(
                    'ability'=>'DESC',
                    'hardWorking'=>'DESC',
                    'sociable'=>'DESC',
                    'davidBowieFan'=>'DESC',
                    'ManUtdSupporter'=>'ASC'
        );
        $this->db->orderBy($orderBy);

        // How many results do we need?
        $this->db->limit(1);

        // Run the search
        $this->db->get();
    }

    protected function _setBenefits(){
        $this->daysHoliday = 28;
        $this->fun         = 'guaranteed';
        $this->salary      = 'negotiable';

    }
}
?>
```

Good news. You only need 5 players.

03

02

55

INTERACTION

01/The Guardian
Placing the card over the poem revealed details of an upcoming interview with former MI5 boss Stella Rimmington in this clever Guardian ad.

02/Road Safety
Advertising was interactive long before the advent of digital. This classic road-safety ad demonstrated the importance of headlights.

The growth of digital has established 'interactive' as a separate category from print, TV, radio and direct mail. But getting consumers to interact with ads has always been an option in traditional media.

Many vintage print ads encouraged readers to engage with the ad itself. An ad for an electric razor showing a smooth pair of legs read, 'To see how good the new Ladyshave is, run your fingers over my legs'. An IBM ad with a picture of a keyboard read, 'To find out how quiet our new typewriter is, tap the keys on this page'. A disturbing ad for child abuse charity NSPCC invited readers to stub out a cigarette on a photo of a baby.

Broadcast advertising has also used interaction. A Canadian radio ad for the homeless shelter Covenant House was played out at a low volume. Anyone who turned up the volume heard a homeless girl's story and the message 'You've just taken the first step to helping street kids – listening'.

The interactive ad has become a dominant form in the age of online. Interactive banners allow users to engage with ads rather than simply clicking through. Since the first of these – a playable version of the game Pong developed for Hewlett-Packard in 1996 – agencies have developed countless inventive variations.

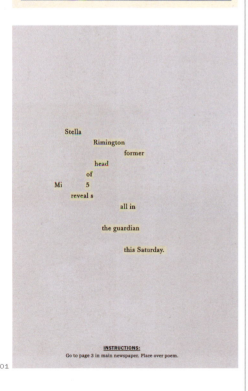

Stella
    Rimington
            former
        head
            of
Mi   5
    reveal s
                all in

        the guardian

            this Saturday.

INSTRUCTIONS:
Go to page 3 in main newspaper. Place over poem.

01

TO MAKE THIS CAR DISAPPEAR, PUT YOUR FINGERS OVER ITS HEADLIGHTS.

Block out the headlights above, and you'll get a good idea of how other drivers see you . if you don't use your headlights on gloomy days.

The fact is they can hardly see you at all. And if you can't be seen, somebody can very easily get hurt.

This is one reason the law says you <u>must</u> put on your headlights when the daylight's poor. You can be fined up to £100 if you don't turn them on in conditions of daytime fog, falling snow, heavy rain or general bad light.

So remember the law. Remember the finger test. And be the bright one.

On gloomy days, put on your headlights.

See and <u>be seen.</u>

IN POOR DAYLIGHT, BE SEEN. YOU MUST USE HEADLIGHTS.

Issued by the Department of the Environment, the Scottish Development Department and the Welsh Office.

02

56

Crowdsourcing allows the general public to create the ads.

CROWDSOURCING

01

With the rise of video sharing and social media, brands have had the option of handing the creative reins over to the public.

The 'Crash the Super Bowl' campaign for Doritos used high-profile media placement as its hook. Members of the public were invited to create ads to run during the Super Bowl. As an extra incentive, a prize of a million dollars was promised if the user-generated ad could top *USA Today*'s Ad Meter. The combination of crowdsourcing and a large cash prize generated huge interest, and the winning ad duly topped the poll.

The PR spin on such work is usually that members of the public have outsmarted ad industry professionals with their fresh ideas. In reality, it's often the method of gathering content that grabs attention, rather than the content itself.

Much as we'd all like to believe that the general public is an untapped source of creative genius, writing ideas takes practice. It's possible but unlikely that you're going to come up with something brilliant and original on your first try. As if to confirm this, a 2010 competition to write a script for the snack Peperami was actually won by two agency creatives.

Rather than asking members of the public to produce advertising ideas, some campaigns encourage them to contribute to existing ones. During the 2012 London Olympics, McDonald's ran the 'We're all making the games' campaign. Video footage submitted by the public was edited into their TV ad, while fan photos ran on digital poster sites.

02

03

57

Ambient ads turn anything into an advertising space, often in clever and unexpected ways.

AMBIENT

01 / Rose Taxis
Ambient ads can appear anywhere. This one for a South African taxi firm ran on the bottom of beer glasses.

02 / Singapore Cancer Society
These lung ashtrays created by the Singapore Cancer Society were an ingenious way to reach smokers.

03 / Bamboo Lingerie
Ads for such small clients as this one began popping up in the nineties. They were sometimes generated by creative departments rather than written in response to a client brief.

Ambient ads appear on unexpected places, such as walls, floors, ceilings, urinals, ticket barriers, petrol pumps, mirrors, benches and anywhere else a brand name and an endline can be stuck.

Ambient has become increasingly important in recent years as a way of reaching customers who avoid conventional advertising, but it's also caused controversy. By making brand messages unavoidable, does it fuel public hostility towards advertising?

As with any other sort of marketing, the public will be much more likely to forgive the intrusion if it's funny or entertaining. Fortunately, this isn't something creatives seem to struggle with. The limitless possibilities of ambient generate ingenious executions year after year.

Another issue with ambient advertising is a legal one. Although some ambient spaces can be bought through conventional channels, others overlap with the illegal practice of flyposting. It's a grey area, and one that puts some clients off.

Ambient ads are often single executions inspired by particular locations, but sometimes they can be extended into campaigns, as with Crispin Porter and Bogusky's ambient ads for the Miami Rescue Mission. Executions included 'bed' written on a park bench and 'closet' written on a shopping trolley. The line was 'When you're homeless, the world looks different'.

01

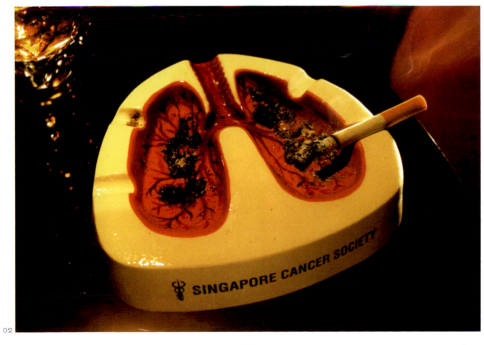

02

03

58

INSTALLATION

Ambient advertising has developed into art installations, sculpture and immersive brand experiences.

As ambient advertising grew more sophisticated, a category developed that went beyond sticking posters in unusual places. Large-scale, immersive 3D brand experiences came to prominence. The ideas for these might come from ad agencies, experiential agencies, PR agencies, online agencies or anyone else on a client's roster.

Nokia used mobile interaction as part of a big-scale event in 2010. They suspended a huge pink arrow from a crane in central London and invited people to text them for directions. The arrow moved to point the right way and displayed the distance in metres.

Human Rights Watch created an ingenious interactive installation in New York's Grand Central Station to promote its campaign to free 2,100 political prisoners in Burma. The installation seemed to show cells containing the prisoners. But the bars of the cells were actually pens that people could remove to sign a petition.

BMW's Kinetic Sculpture in its own museum in Munich blurs the boundaries between art and advertising further. It consists of 714 aluminium balls moved by computer-controlled motors. The balls move chaotically at first, but then begin to trace out the shapes of various BMW cars.

01 / BMW

This Kinetic Sculpture in the BMW Museum in Munich traces out the shapes of vehicles with aluminium balls.

02 / Nokia

Nokia suspended a huge arrow above central London in 2010. Anyone passing could ask it to point the direction to somewhere.

03 / Human Rights Watch

The bars of the prison cells in this installation for Human Rights Watch are actually pens. People were asked to remove the pens to sign a petition.

01

02

03

59

SPECIAL BUILDS

Before ambient took off as a category, special-build posters were the showcase for innovative outdoor advertising. Special builds include any unconventional use of poster sites, such as adding objects to them, forming them into different shapes and making them out of unusual materials.

Special builds can encompass anything from the Prudential poster 'I want to be able to make ends meet', which was made to look as though it had been pasted up incorrectly, to the Araldite ad that showed off the strength of the adhesive by sticking a car to a billboard.

Objects can be added to posters to create special builds. An *Economist* poster featured a giant light bulb that lit up as people walked underneath. A McDonald's poster featured a sundial that moved from the breakfast to the lunch menu as the morning passed. DDB Düsseldorf built a horizontal poster to advertise a convertible VW. When the sun came out, the shadow cast by the poster would form the words 'Perfect day for a test drive'.

Sometimes a special build can be based around unusual poster materials. Environmental organization Friends of the Earth printed a poster on litmus paper so it would turn red to highlight the amount of acid in rainwater. The line was, 'This is litmus paper. When acid rain is falling, you should see red.'

Another type of special build deliberately tampers with a poster site to make it look faulty. An ad for South African electricity suppliers Eskom turned on just one of the four floodlights above the billboard site. The line underneath the functioning light was, 'Use electricity wisely'.

01 / McDonald's
You don't always have to use new technology to make an innovative ad. This McDonald's special build used a piece of technology that's thousands of years old – the sundial.

02 / VW
This VW ad would only work on sunny days. If the sun shone through the poster, its shadow would read, 'Perfect day for a test drive'.

03 / The Economist
The light bulb on this Economist poster lit up whenever someone walked underneath.

01

02

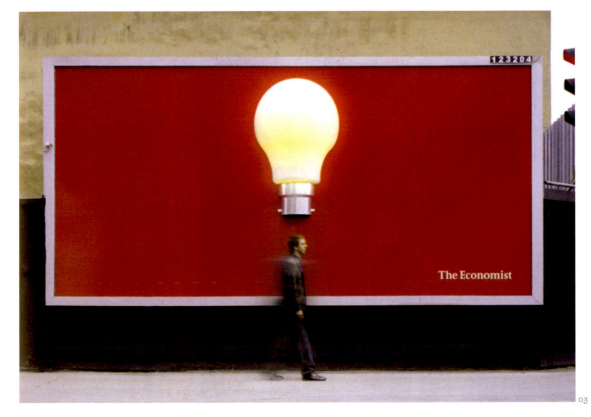

03

60

High-profile events can generate media coverage worth millions.

STUNTS

High-profile events that attract press and online attention are increasingly important as the line between ads and content blurs. Traditionally the responsibility of PR agencies, stunts can now come from anyone on a client's roster.

Sometimes an ad is so unusual it becomes a PR event in itself. In 2007 Deadline Express Couriers built an exploding billboard in Auckland, New Zealand. The poster featured a clock counting down to a time when it would self-destruct. The endline underneath read, 'When we give you a time, we mean it'. The poster received coverage on TV, in press and online, and a large crowd turned out to watch it explode.

An unusual recruitment campaign became the basis of one of the most successful PR stunts of recent years. Tourism Queensland ran a campaign looking for someone to take on 'the best job in the world', namely caretaker on Australia's Hamilton Island. From just a few small-space recruitment ads, the campaign ballooned into a high-profile event, covered in print and on TV around the world.

When Felix Baumgartner jumped from the edge of space in the 'Red Bull Stratos' event, much was made of the records he broke. It was the highest altitude jump in history, and Baumgartner became the first person to break the sound barrier without engine power. But it was also a record-breaking stunt for sponsors Red Bull. The jump was watched by 7 million people live on YouTube, setting the record for live-stream viewership. Meanwhile, the event was being discussed on Twitter and Facebook, and getting covered on TV news bulletins worldwide. Encompassing sponsorship, branded content, social media and PR stunt, Baumgartner's jump brought Red Bull to the attention of hundreds of millions around the world.

01

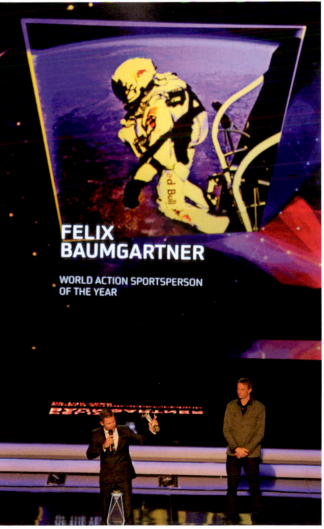

01 / Deadline Express Couriers
This Deadline Express Couriers poster turned a special build into a PR stunt by counting down to a moment of destruction.

02 / Tourism Queensland
Tourism Queensland's 'Best job in the world' campaign received global coverage estimated to be worth over $150 million.

03 / Red Bull Stratos
Red Bull Stratos, Felix Baumgartner's jump from the edge of space in 2012, brought unprecedented coverage for his sponsor.

61

The physical properties of magazines, newspapers and poster sites can be used in clever ways.

USING THE MEDIUM

You don't always need elaborate special builds or inserts to come up with a novel use of print media. Some ads use the physical properties of magazines and posters inventively.

Many double-page magazine ads make clever use of their format. An Adidas ad showed a woman holding weights on either side so that it looked like she was lifting them as you pulled the pages open. A campaign for WMF knives showed fine slices of fish, chicken and lobster on either side of the spread so that opening the page seemed to make them fall apart. An ad for Nimble low-calorie bread showed a horizontal woman's torso with the belt along the gutter so that the curve of the page looked like a roll of fat.

An ad for Vapona fly spray printed a flat version of the packaging on the back of a magazine, so it could be rolled up to resemble the can.

A newspaper ad for Crimestoppers printed a photo of a knife on the back page of a newspaper so it looked as though whoever was holding the paper was carrying a knife. A phone number was given out underneath to report genuine knife carriers.

Posters can also refer to the physical space they occupy. An ad for the Australian Office of Road Safety used poster sites on either side of a bus stop to clever effect. The first poster read, 'At 60 km/h you'd stop about here'. The second poster read, 'At 65 km/h you'd stop about here'. The endline was, 'Drop 5. Save lives.'

01

02

03

62

HOAXES

Elaborate practical jokes are sometimes developed on behalf of brands.

Making deliberately false claims in an ad as a practical joke is most common on April Fools' Day, when brands will pretend to do things like launch a strange new product.

Sometimes entire campaigns can be built around a hoax. A Canadian campaign for the Richmond Savings Credit Union ran ads from a fictional organization called the 'Humongous Bank'. The true client was only revealed in the small print below.

Digital Kitchen's campaign for the HBO show *True Blood* took the technique a step further by using real brands in hoax ads. The campaign imagined how brands would market to vampires if they were real. Posters from Mini, Harley-Davidson, Geico, Ecko and Monster.com targeted bloodsuckers directly, and drove people to the *True Blood* website.

Hoaxes have proliferated in the age of online. As with print ads and press releases, a lot of activity is based around April Fools' Day. Fake tweets and Facebook updates might be fairly expected now, but hoaxes in other places can still surprise. On 1 April 2010, a sexy cheerleader appeared on Chatroulette with instructions such as 'Be a doggy, get a dance'. Those who played along were rewarded with a dance from a skinny old man in a cheerleader outfit. The cheerleader than reappeared with a 'Happy April Fools' Day from Dr Pepper' sign.

We built this bank one service charge at a time.

HUMUNGOUS BANK*

Your money is our money.

*If you think the big bucks are getting bigger at your expense, it's time you talked to Richmond Savings. We believe in rewarding our customers with fewer charges. Not to mention service that's second to none. After all, that's how we built our business. We're not a bank. We're better.

01

02

01 / Richmond Savings
A refreshingly honest ad for a bank? This hoax campaign from Richmond Savings highlighted the difference between banks and credit unions.

02 / Dr Pepper
Teenage boys must have thought their dreams had come true when a sexy cheerleader appeared on Chatroulette. But it was all part of a hoax from Dr Pepper.

03 / True Blood
A billboard targeting blood-sucking fiends? This campaign for the HBO show *True Blood* used real brands as part of the gag.

03

63

HIDDEN CAMERA

Some campaigns use concealed cameras to capture the reactions of genuine members of the public.

When Allen Funt's radio series 'Candid Microphone' transferred to TV and changed its name to 'Candid Camera', a new comic genre was born. Practical jokes were played on unsuspecting members of the public, with concealed cameras capturing the results. The format has been used in advertising many times since.

As part of its anti-smoking campaign, Arnold Worldwide staged a series of fake job interviews to find out if candidates had what it took to work at a company called 'Big Tobacco'. We see one candidate being asked if they're prepared to plead the fifth, like one tobacco delegate did 97 times during a deposition. We see another being quizzed on his skills at spinning bad news. And we see another reacting to the news that the tobacco industry kills 5 million people a year. The practical jokes gave fresh urgency to a message that's been exhausted by shock advertising over the years.

A 2007 campaign for Coke Zero was based around the conceit that it tastes so much like Coke that marketing execs of the original variety wanted to sue it for 'taste infringement'. The ads showed Coke execs asking real lawyers how a company would go about suing itself.

The flashmobbing trend of the noughties, where people would gather in a public place to act out a scene, had an obvious influence on hidden-camera advertising. A 2009 ad for T-Mobile showed people congregating in a train station to perform a synchronized dance routine while surprised members of the public looked on.

01 / Big Tobacco
These anti-smoking ads took the form of spoof interviews for a job at a fictitious company called 'Big Tobacco'.

02 / Coke Zero
This hidden-camera prank was based around the idea that Classic Coke wanted to sue Coke Zero because it tasted too similar.

03 / T-Mobile
This ad for T-Mobile showed people meeting in a train station to perform a dance routine. It was inspired by the contemporary flashmobbing trend.

01

02

03

64

DOCUMENTARY

Lots of TV ads are referred to as having a 'documentary' style. This can mean anything from naturalistic performances shot with handheld cameras to footage of real people going about their lives.

Chrysler's 2013 Super Bowl spot generated a lot of discussion by using documentary photography in a high-profile timeslot. Agency The Richards Group briefed ten photographers to visit farmers and shoot them working and resting. The best shots were edited to radio broadcaster Paul Harvey's 'So God made a farmer' speech. The result was a tone of stark authenticity that took attention away from effects-laden spectaculars and high-profile endorsements.

Documentary photography is an option in print advertising too. A campaign to promote Terminal 5 of London's Heathrow Airport showed genuine travellers and described their hassle-free journeys. It was produced in response to negative reports about long queues and cancelled flights.

In the past, attempts to shoot genuine footage and edit it down to 30- or 60-second time lengths were often unsatisfying, but online has opened up new possibilities for documentary advertising. In 2007, a campaign for Speight's Ale shipped an entire pub over from New Zealand to England to quench the thirst of homesick ex-pats. The journey and arrival were documented in a live weblog, and footage made its way on to news stations around the world.

Spoof documentaries have become a popular format in comedy, following TV shows such as *The Office*. Crispin Porter and Bogusky's 'Counterfeit Mini' campaign was an original take on this well-worn format. Purporting to be a documentary exposing a black market of counterfeit Mini Coopers, it was actually a clever way of highlighting the qualities of the car.

01

01 / Mini
Spoof documentaries
have become popular
in films and on TV.
This campaign purports
to investigate the illegal
trade in counterfeit
Mini Coopers.

02 / Speight's
In 2007 Speight's
shipped an alehouse
all the way from New
Zealand to England
and documented the
journey online.

03 / Terminal 5
Documentary
photography and
descriptions of genuine
events were used to
promote Heathrow
Airport's Terminal 5
shortly after it opened.

02

03

65

BIG ADS

01 / British Airways
This 1989 'Face' ad from British Airways set the tone for epic ads with hundreds of extras.

02 / Guinness
This Guinness ad turned an entire Argentinian town into a domino rally as part of the 'Good things come to those who wait' campaign.

03 / Chanel No 5
Reported to be the most expensive ad ever made, Baz Luhrmann's Chanel No 5 spot lasts three minutes and stars Nicole Kidman.

'It's a big ad!' sang the cast of the 2005 Carlton Draught spoof. 'It's just so freaking huge.' It came after a couple of decades when brands seemed to be competing to see who could spend the most on an event commercial.

The 'big ad' most directly referenced by the Carlton Draught parody was probably British Airway's 'Face' spot from 1989. The ad, which was directed by Hugh Hudson, shows an aerial shot of hundreds of people gathering to form a face, which winks at the camera. The face turns into a globe and we see the slogan 'The world's favourite airline'.

The 2007 'Tipping Point' ad for Guinness turned an entire Argentinian town into a domino rally as fridges, cases, cars and wardrobes toppled over before culminating in a huge pint.

'Tipping Point' was alleged to have cost $16 million, but it still wasn't the most expensive ad ever made. That title is thought to belong to Baz Luhrmann's 'No 5 the Film' for Chanel No 5, which had a reputed price tag of $33 million. The 180-second spot stars Nicole Kidman as a famous actress who falls in love with a writer, and has a similar style to Luhrmann's 'Red Curtain' trilogy.

01

GOOD THINGS COME TO THOSE WHO WAIT.

guinnesstipping.com

02

03

66

Brand-sponsored content has blurred the lines between advertising and entertainment.

BRANDED CONTENT

01 / Target
Target's short film, *Falling for You*, featured items that could be selected from a scrolling sidebar.

02 / The Dearborn Independent
Branded content is nothing new. Henry Ford bought the Dearborn Independent in 1919 and used it to promote his motor company. Unfortunately, he also used it to promote his anti-Semitic views.

03 / Somers Town
The Shane Meadows film *Somers Town* was funded by Eurostar. It featured the train, but branding was subtle.

Entertainment created by brands is nothing new. From Michelin Guides to Henry Ford's newspaper the *Dearborn Independent* to the radio serials of the 1930s, which were dubbed 'soap operas' due to their sponsors, the distinction between advertising and entertainment has always been an uncertain one. But it's a distinction that's become increasingly blurred as technology has made it easier for consumers to avoid traditional ads.

In 2006, Axe Dry funded an hour-long TV special called *The Gamekillers*, which was based on its ad campaign at the time. The show featured comic characters called 'gamekillers' ruining the dates of real-life couples in hidden-camera stunts. It proved so popular that a follow-up series was commissioned.

Branded content hit the big screen in 2008 with the film *Somers Town*, which was directed by Shane Meadows. The film was funded by Eurostar, the high-speed railway connecting London and Paris. Although the train formed part of the story, the film featured no overt branding.

A less subtle variation on branded content was Target's *Falling for You*, a romantic comedy that was dubbed the first ever 'shoppable film'. Online viewers could see a scrolling sidebar next to the film that displayed the items featured in it. They could click to 'favourite' them as they were watching, and at the end they could review their choices and decide which ones to purchase.

01

02

03

67

PLAYING WITH THE LOGO

Basing an ad around a logo might not seem especially lateral, but it can create simple and clever ads.

It's sometimes possible to crack a brief with just a minor alteration to a logo. In the UK, the last ever episode of the sitcom *Friends* ran on a Friday. The poster rearranged the show's logo to read, 'ENDS FRI'. Hats off to the creatives for spotting that one.

The McDonald's 'golden arches' logo has a simplicity that's allowed it to be used as a visual simile for things such as mustard on a hotdog and the string of a basketball net. When the restaurant ran a topical poster to mark the new millennium, two logos were placed side by side to spell out 'MM', the year 2000 in Roman numerals.

An ad for Carlsberg that warned against Christmas drink-driving featured just the 'lsberg' part of the logo. The line read, 'Have a great Christmas. Leave the car at home.'

When Adidas were opening a store in Manchester, a city that's famous for its bad weather, the brand's three-stripe logo was transformed into a neat visual simile for rain.

Playing with a logo will not lead to an elegant solution for every brief. But it's a technique that can be very satisfying when it works.

01/Adidas
The Adidas logo is used to suggest rain in this ad to promote a store opening in notoriously showery city Manchester.

02/Holsten Pils
This campaign for Holsten Pils used a series of anagrams of the brand name, including 'Tells on hips', 'Spot ill hens' and 'Tonsils help'.

03/Channel 4
In the UK, the last ever episode of *Friends* aired on a Friday. You'd have kicked yourself if you'd worked on the brief and missed this.

adidas manchester

68

Symbols can be a good shortcut to communicating a benefit. Used properly, they can create incredibly simple advertising.

SYMBOLS

The 'Infinity' ad for Bic pens by TBWA\Hunt\Lascaris Johannesburg is a brilliant example of how a symbol can be used to communicate a proposition. It manages to be both a rewarding visual and a convincing product demonstration without using a single word.

Sometimes a product can be arranged or altered to resemble a symbol. A poster in the long-running 'Have a break' campaign placed two Kit Kat fingers side by side to create the 'pause' symbol.

Public signage contains plenty of symbols that can be appropriated, such as the ones to do with road travel and public transport. This is somewhat well-worn territory, and it's easy to slip into cliché. But signs can still make for arresting visuals with a fresh enough twist. An ad in Volkswagen's 'Surprisingly ordinary prices' campaign reproduced the 'risk of shock' symbol above the price of a Polo L.

One way to avoid familiarity is to use the new symbols that events and technology bring to prominence. An Australian McDonald's ad arranged French fries into the shape of the Wi-Fi symbol to promote the offer of free web access.

01

02 / **Bic**
If a proposition is simple enough to be expressed as a symbol, it can make for wonderfully clean ads. This Bic ad doesn't need to use any words at all.

03 / **Kit Kat**
Sometimes the product can be transformed into a symbol. This ad turns the bars of a Kit Kat into a visual simile for the 'pause' symbol.

02

Have a break. Have a KitKat

03

69

Some ads feature clever use of type as the main element.

TYPOGRAPHY

01 / Penguin
Smaller type can be used to create shapes. This Malaysian ad for Penguin Audiobooks turns words into soundwaves.

02 / Museum of Childhood
The type in this ad for the Museum of Childhood is created from classic toys such as Slinkys, Scalextric tracks and Rubik's Cubes.

03 / Virgin Atlantic
The letters making up the plane spell out 'soon' in Arabic in this Virgin Atlantic ad. Even if you can't read Arabic, the letters still make an intriguing visual.

A particular variety of visual simile that's popular in advertising and design agencies is the 'type ad', where letters are arranged to look like objects, or objects are arranged to look like letters.

The type ad can be a useful option for press ads, as it can often be created in-house by graphic designers.

AMV's 'Memory back guarantee with every visit' ad for the Museum of Childhood is a good example. Every letter in the headline is created by a retro toy, turning the ad into an enjoyable puzzle.

Type ads can work in any language. A poster for Virgin Atlantic announcing flights to Dubai arranged the Arabic word for 'soon' into the shape of a plane.

Blocks of type can also be arranged to make shapes. An ad for Penguin Audiobooks from Young & Rubicam Kuala Lumpur arranged passages from books into soundwaves. The line was, 'Hear your favourite books'.

On television and online, 'kinetic typography' ads animate words, often as they're said in voiceover. The godfather of kinetic typography was Saul Bass, whose title sequences to films such as Alfred Hitchcock's *North by Northwest* used moving text in startlingly inventive ways.

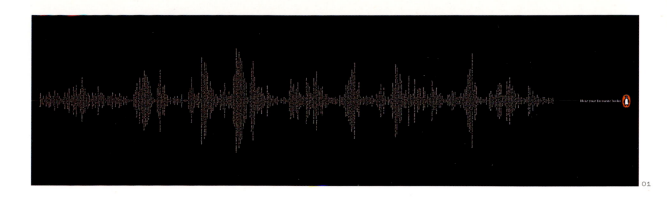

70

PRICING

01/BA
Good design can help price ads stand out. The endline of this campaign was, 'Our most attractive prices'.

02/VW
Volkswagen's 'Surprisingly ordinary prices' campaign played on the idea that the prices were so low you had to be careful when reading them.

Most brands will require ads that focus on price at some point. But how can price ads stand out from the thousands of other special offers that clutter billboards, banners and TV screens?

Some ads draw attention to price in novel or unexpected ways. Volkswagen's 'Surprisingly ordinary prices' campaign used the conceit that the prices were dangerous to read. An underground poster read, 'For your safety: Please stand back from edge of platform' above the price of the Polo car. Another poster gave out the number of the St John Ambulance service as well as the price.

Tesco's 'Every little helps' campaign developed a friendly, informal tone for their pricing ads, which often play with figures of speech. An example was, 'Soap. 24p. See, the more we sell, the less we charge. You scratch our back. We gently exfoliate yours.'

Distinctive art direction can make price ads more distinctive too. British Airways ran a campaign of beautifully designed prices with the line 'Our most attractive prices'. Focusing on one price at a time, the ads stood out from the rushed, crowded competition.

Interestingly, French supermarket Carrefour's Malaysian operation managed to grab attention by doing the exact opposite. They cluttered a price ad so much that it resembled an intricate work of art – a very inventive way to communicate the 'low prices storewide' message.

from **£34**

BORDEAUX one-way

OUR MOST ATTRACTIVE PRICES AT **ba.com**

FOR YOUR SAFETY:

Please stand back from edge of platform.

Polo L £7990.

Surprisingly ordinary prices VW

02

71

COMPETITIVE ADS

Avis is only No.2 in rent a cars. So why go with us?

We try harder.
(When you're not the biggest, you have to.)
We just can't afford dirty ash-trays. Or half-empty gas tanks. Or worn wipers. Or unwashed cars. Or low tires. Or anything less than seat-adjusters that adjust. Heaters that heat. Defrosters that defrost.
Obviously, the thing we try hardest for is just to be nice. To start you out right with a new car, like a lively, super-torque Ford, and a pleasant smile. To know, say, where you get a good pastrami sandwich in Duluth. Why?
Because we can't afford to take you for granted. Go with us next time.
The line at our counter is shorter.

01

Competitive advertising, sometimes also called 'comparative advertising', explicitly compares a brand to a rival. It's highly controversial, and is subject to restrictions in many countries.

Many famous rival brands have taken each other on through competitive ads. The console wars of the eighties and nineties saw lines such as 'Genesis does what Nintendon't'. Apple's 'Mac vs PC' campaign caused a million techie debates in the noughties. And the 'cola wars' between Pepsi and Coke in the eighties were deemed important enough to be referenced in Billy Joel's 'We Didn't Start the Fire'.

Perhaps the most famous competitive campaign was 'We try harder' for Avis car rental in 1963. The ads took the unprecedented step of admitting the brand was trailing its main rival, and making a virtue of it. With ingenious logic, the ads made Hertz look like complacent market leaders and positioned Avis as the plucky underdog. The brand's hard-working target audience identified with the positioning, and the campaign was a huge success.

Competitive advertising comes under close scrutiny during political campaigns. The most notorious political ad is probably the 'Daisy' commercial created for Lyndon B. Johnson by DDB. The ad showed a young girl picking the petals off a daisy in a field. When her count reaches nine, her voice is replaced by a male voice counting down to zero and we cut to a missile launch. The voiceover says, 'Vote for President Johnson on November 3rd. The stakes are too high for you to stay home.'

02

01 / Avis
This classic DDB campaign positioned Avis as the plucky underdog and Hertz as the smug establishment. It was an important part of the creative revolution of the sixties.

02 / Daisy
Competitive ads used in political campaigns can become very famous. This DDB ad for Lyndon B. Johnson showed a little girl and a nuclear explosion.

03 / FedEx
Competitive campaigns often refer to their rivals directly, as in this cheeky FedEx ad from BBDO Düsseldorf.

Range ads communicate the breadth of a product or service.

72

RANGE

01 / Dulux
'You pick it, we'll match it'. This in-store ad for Dulux was an inventive way of communicating range. You could peel away any part of the poster, take it to the counter and ask them to match the colour.

02 / Observer Music Monthly
'From Abba to Zappa'. Mother created 26 music-themed icons in this range ad for the *Observer Music Monthly*.

Like the price ad, the 'range' ad is something that most creatives will be asked to come up with at some point. It can often be hard, though, to produce a simple visual while demonstrating the breadth of a service or product.

One obvious answer is to choose two disparate things as examples of the range. The two items can then be mashed up into a single image. Business telephone directory the Yellow Pages ran a campaign to prove how comprehensive their listings were. Images of a frog and a frogman were fused to represent diving classes and French restaurants.

Other ads find clever ways to showcase an entire range in a single ad. Mother's campaign for the *Observer Music Monthly* designed 26 icons of artists to show their offering 'From Abba to Zappa'. Working out whom the icons represented added an enjoyable puzzle for music fans.

Dulux's 'You pick it, we'll match it' campaign demonstrated the huge variety of colours the paint comes in. In-store posters were made from stickers you could peel away and take to the counter. It was a good example of a campaign that managed to communicate a range proposition in a single image.

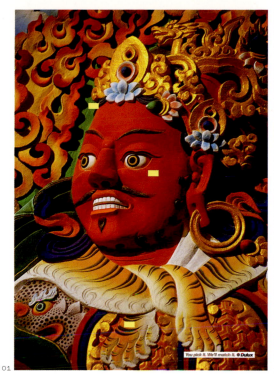

01

02

73

PRODUCT DEMONSTRATION

01

Product demonstration is one of the most basic forms of advertising. Showing off the features of a product to camera might be associated with daytime infomercials and very early TV ads but there's something satisfying about product-demo ads that manage to entertain too.

Many celebrated TV ads have been product demonstrations. Lego's 'Kipper' ad created stop-motion animation of the bricks themselves to show the unique adaptability of the toy. A very famous product demo for VW asked, 'Have you ever wondered what the man who drives a snowplow drives to the snowplow?' And an ad for American Tourister suitcases showed a gorilla giving the product hell while a voiceover described the threats of 'ruthless porters, savage baggage masters and all butter-fingered baggage handlers'.

Demonstration ads don't always have to use pristine product shots. A Volvo press ad showed a car after a crash and the line 'We design every Volvo to look like this'. The ad was highlighting the car's safety cage, which protects passengers in accidents.

Product demos don't have to lead to old-fashioned, conventional layouts either. A press ad for file-compression software Stuffit Deluxe condensed hundreds of images into one, creating a visually distinct ad.

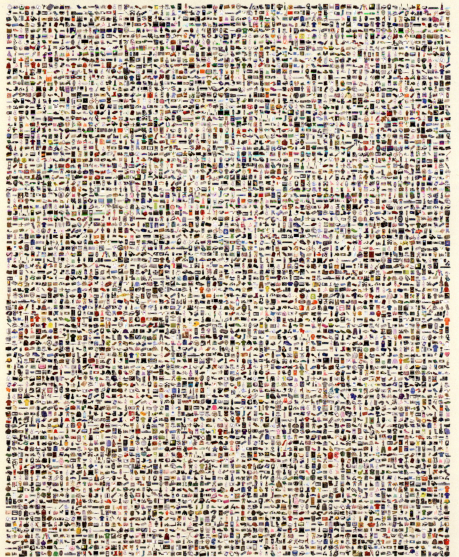

This press ad was adapted from a famous sixties TV spot that showed a snowplough driver going to work in a VW. A beautifully simple product demonstration.

02 / **Stuffit Deluxe**
Product demos don't have to be old-fashioned. This ad for Stuffit Deluxe software showed off its file-compression capabilities in a visually imaginative way.

03 / **American Tourister**
Who better than a gorilla to torture-test a suitcase? Lots of classic TV ads have been product demonstrations.

03

74

PRODUCT SHOT

The old maxim 'Expand the mandatory' dictates that you should base your ad around the thing that's most important to your client. A good example is the 'product shot'. Sometimes clients want the product to be so big it overwhelms all the other elements of a print ad. In these cases it is often best to make the product the main visual.

So how do you make a product-shot ad interesting? There's a chance you might not need to do anything, of course. You might be highlighting a new gadget that consumers will be genuinely interested to look at, for example. But it's more likely that you'll need to find a way to reward people for looking at the ad.

Writing a witty headline to go with the visual is probably the simplest way, but there might also be a clever way to shoot the product. An ad for Heinz Spiderman pasta shapes showed the tin upside down in a cupboard, as if it had the powers of the superhero himself. An ad for the listings guide that comes free with British newspaper *The Guardian* showed the product virtually destroyed from overuse.

A Budweiser ad in the 'King of beers' campaign turned the bottle top upside down to create a smart visual simile. An add for Hellmann's extra light mayonnaise showed the label slipping down to the bottom of the jar as if the product itself had slimmed down.

There might not always be a solution as simple as these, but it's worth remembering that embracing the product shot can lead to good advertising too.

01 / Heinz

Spiderman pasta shapes are given the powers of Peter Parker's alter ego in this ad from Leo Burnett London.

02 / Budweiser

'The king of beers.' This Budweiser ad is both a product shot and a visual simile. A neat trick if you can make it work.

03 / Hellmann's

The jar itself seems to have lost weight in this simple ad for Hellman's extra light mayonnaise.

01

02

03

75

Showing customer reactions to free samples is a traditional type of advertising, but it can be executed in a fresh way.

PRODUCT SAMPLING

01 / Burger King
Burger King's 'Whopper Virgins' campaign took the Whopper and the Big Mac to some of the world's remotest people.

02 / Oasis
New Yorkers got to sample new Oasis songs in 2008 through buskers. The band taught their songs to street musicians prior to the release of their new album.

03 / National Gallery
Sampling can work well for unexpected products. This campaign for London's National Gallery reproduced famous artworks on the street.

Giving away freebies to customers in shopping malls and supermarkets can be an effective way of promoting a product. Customer reactions to free samples can then be made into ads.

Sampling and taste tests have featured in such classic campaigns as the 'Pepsi Challenge'. This was a test in which ordinary members of the public were blindfolded and asked to sip two different types of cola. According to the campaign, the majority of participants selected Pepsi.

Although such ads might seem outmoded now, a few recent campaigns have revived sampling and taste tests for modern audiences.

Burger King's 'Whopper Virgins' campaign attempted to create the 'world's purest taste test' by getting people from remote places who'd never tasted burgers before to compare the Whopper and the Big Mac. It was an innovate twist on sampling ads, though some accused the campaign of cultural imperialism.

The rise of ambient and online have led to some unusual products taking a sampling approach. London's National Gallery launched its 'Grand Tour' campaign in 2007. It placed reproductions of the gallery's most famous works around the city, together with plaques and a number to phone for an audio guide. The following year, rock band Oasis launched their *Dig Out Your Soul* album by letting buskers on the streets of New York perform the songs before the album was released.

01

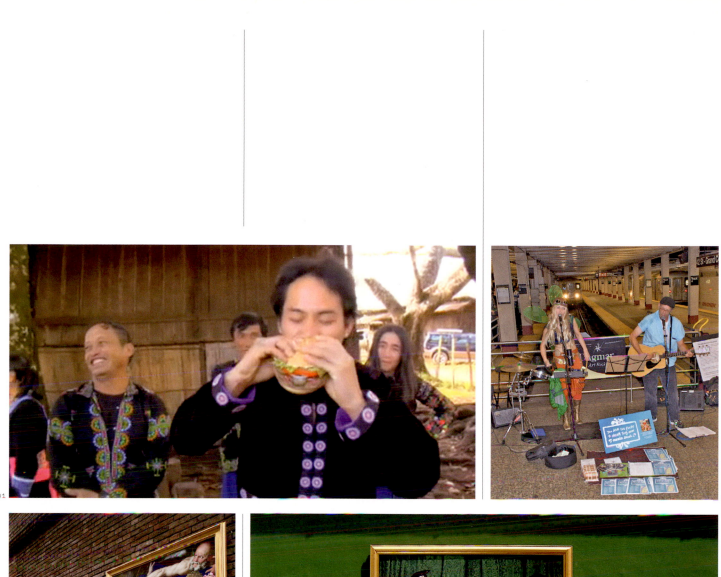

02

03

76

TOPICAL

Referring to topical events can make for cheeky, entertaining ads. If agencies spot an overlap between a news story and an endline, they'll often try and get a topical ad running.

Topical ads are often presented as a story ripped from a newspaper with an endline underneath. In 2004 Britney Spears wed her childhood friend Jason Alexander and then had the marriage annulled a day later. The story fitted perfectly with the '24 hour Lynx effect' campaign, and a topical ad was put together.

Package holiday firm Club 18–30 cheekily hijacked the confusion following the 2000 US presidential election. The brand's association with holiday sex was so established that they only needed to add their logo to a shot of a man holding a 'We want Bush' placard.

A similar type of execution, often called a 'tactical ad', is created to coincide with an upcoming event such as Christmas or an election. Unlike topical ads, tactical ads allow agencies more time to craft and produce ideas.

For the 2008 US presidential election, Jack Daniels ran a series of posters using the type and iconography of classic political posters. To add authenticity, they were produced on antique printmaking equipment.

Wieden and Kennedy Portland's Nike spot for 1 January 2000 was an especially inventive tactical ad. Directed by Spike Jonze, the ad shows a world in which all the pessimistic predictions about the year 2000 and the millennium bug have come true. As riots rage in the streets, tanks roll in and rockets fly overhead, a man in Nike trainers jogs dutifully on. Even this level of chaos can't stop him from just doing it.

01

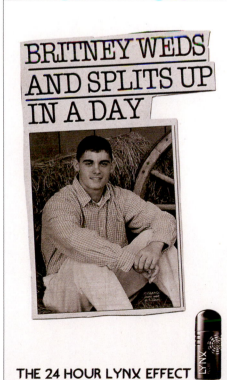

BRITNEY WEDS AND SPLITS UP IN A DAY

THE 24 HOUR LYNX EFFECT

01 / Nike
The apocalyptic predictions for the turn of the millennium came true in this tactical Nike spot, which ran on 1 January 2000.

02 / Lynx
The classic format of the topical ad. A story that appears to have been torn from a newspaper is presented alongside the brand's current endline.

03 / Jack Daniels
Jack Daniels ran tactical posters during the 2008 US presidential election. They were printed using suitably old-fashioned methods.

With all due respect to DEMOCRACY there's still a place for BENEVOLENT DICTATORSHIPS

JACK DANIEL PROPRIETOR

Socialize liberally. OLD N°7 BRAND Drink conservatively.

77

PUZZLES

Plenty of ads use formats that require readers to decode some sort of puzzle, along the lines of long-running game show 'Catch Phrase'. But some campaigns deliberately appropriate other forms of puzzle.

As with all ads that require close attention, the reader needs to be rewarded. Saatchi & Saatchi New York's campaign for 42 Below Vodka featured rows of retro clip art. At first it seems that the ads are deliberately surreal or obscure. But if you look at the pictures in order, they tell humourous stories about nights gone wrong, famous people and even bizarre science fiction.

Stella Artois promoted its film sponsorship with ads that contained hidden clues to over 20 films each. They ranged from obvious references to Alfred Hitchcock's *The Birds* to subtler allusions to *Donnie Darko* and *The Exorcist*.

Some ads attempt to quiz readers with trivia questions. Sometimes these can be compelling enough to drive readers to a website for answers. Transport for London ran a campaign of 'Tube or false' teasers, such as 'Only two tube stations have all five vowels in their names', and their site revealed the answers. In this case the statement was true, and the underground stations in question were Mansion House and South Ealing.

01 / **Stella Artois**
How many movie references can you spot in this ad for Stella Artois? Readers will spend lots of time engaging in puzzle ads if they're well executed.

02 / **42 Below Vodka**
This campaign for 42 Below Vodka told cryptic stories in retro clip art.

03 / **Transport for London**
This Transport for London campaign ran true or false questions about their underground trains and revealed the answers online.

01

classic films
coming soon to a town near you

buy a stella artois this summer and you could instantly win a classic film on dvd. but that's not all.
you could also win vip tickets to an exclusive screening of 'birdman of alcatraz' on alcatraz island itself.
a little extravagant? perhaps. but being frugal has never been our forte.

02

A SECTION OF THE ROMAN CITY
WALLS CAN STILL BE SEEN INSIDE
TOWER HILL STATION

MAYOR OF LONDON

Tube or False?
Find out at tfl.gov.uk/tubeorfalse

Transport for London UNDERGROUND

03

78

ILLUSION

01 / Ariel
The stain is actually placed a few feet in front of this Ariel poster. As you drive past, it seems to remove itself from the shirt.

02 / Oxy
Focus on the bottle of Oxy acne treatment in this ad and the spots around it will disappear — an illusion that delivers a clever pun.

03 / PlayStation
If you were close to this PlayStation poster, it might have looked like a random jumble of symbols. But seen from a distance, it resembled eyes.

Optical illusions trick our brains, making still images seem to move or flat images seem to have depth. They invite attention, so it's no surprise that advertising has made use of them.

Ogilvy South Africa's ad for spot treatment Oxy uses a type of visual illusion that makes you focus on a central spot while colours around it disappear. In this case, it's a bottle you have to focus on to make the spots around it disappear, creating a neat visual pun.

A similar disappearing act was used in a roadside billboard for Ariel detergent in Argentina. A cut-out of a stain was placed on a pole a few feet in front of a poster displaying a white shirt and the line 'Disappears easily'. From a distance, it looked as though the stain was on the shirt. But as you drove past, the stain seemed to move away, leaving just the clean shirt.

TBWA London's PlayStation campaign featured the console's four symbols in place of a conventional logo. This allowed them to run a poster that looked like a confusing jumble of shapes if you were close up, but resembled a pair of eyes if seen from the other side of the street. This is the kind of cryptic approach that can work well for a brand with a cult following.

01

02

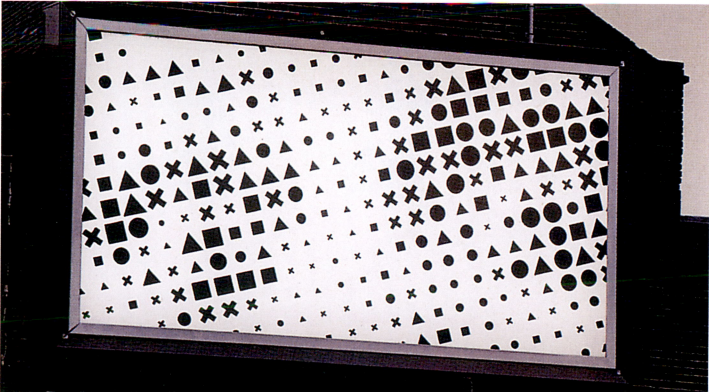

03

79

DIAGRAMS

While some might think they make rather unremarkable visuals, diagrams can in fact be used to create entertaining ads.

Venn diagrams, bar charts and flow charts are often used as a humorously serious way of presenting trivial information. A campaign for German insurance company DEVK used Venn diagrams to tell stories about accidents. One was about getting teeth knocked out by a nightclub bouncer while another was about a collision between a cyclist and motorist caused by a woman wearing a mini-skirt.

A campaign to announce the annual Sunday Times Rich List used mathematical symbols to demonstrate the wealth of famous people. Four Simon Cowells were worth one Andrew Lloyd Webber, while two Alan Sugars, four Roman Abramovichs and two Bernie Ecclestones were all put together to equal one Bill Gates.

Certain products or services might have types of diagrams associated with them. An Ogilvy South Africa campaign for ESPN showed seating charts for baseball, boxing and basketball with an illustration of a sofa in place of front-row seats. It was a simple way of reminding viewers that good sports coverage put them right in the action, and it made for an original ad.

01 / ESPN

Diagrams can lead
to simple, wordless
communication, as
with this Ogilvy South
Africa campaign for
sports channel ESPN.

02 / Sunday Times

This campaign for the
Sunday Times Rich
List showed the kind
of maths that everyone
wants to know about.

03 / DEVK

A Venn diagram for
an insurance company
might not sound like
anyone's idea of fun, but
this DEVK campaign
told engaging stories.

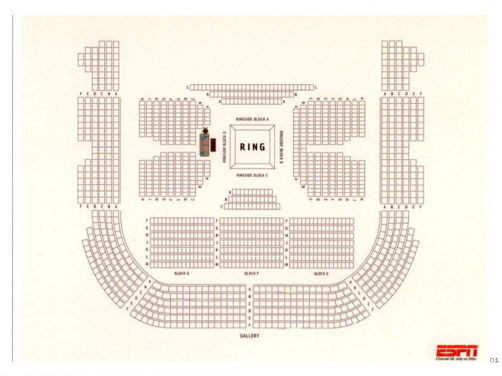

01

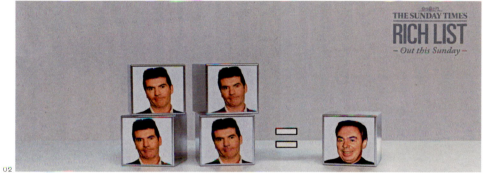

02

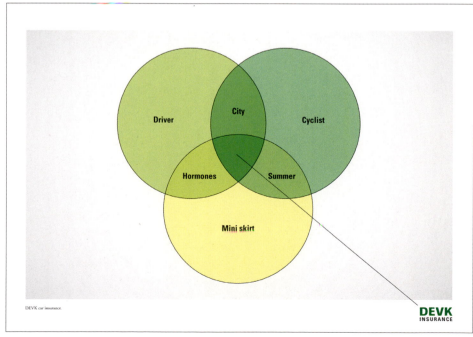

03

80

ANNOTATION

Copy is sometimes laid over visuals as a series of annotations instead of a separate element, such as a headline.

A press campaign for Adidas annotated pictures to give an insight into the mind of a jogger. One ad showed a street stretching out ahead, with lines like 'Just to the signpost', 'Just to the car' and 'Just to the kerb' over the top. Rather than simply claiming the brand knows how runners feel, the ad proves it by showing us their thoughts.

Annotating visuals to promote the written word might seem strange, but Saatchi & Saatchi Malaysia's campaign for Penguin Books evokes the excitement of reading very effectively. Scenes such as a body at the bottom of a stairwell and a husband coming home to catch his adulterous wife are annotated with page numbers, letting us work out the sequence of events.

A series of inserts created by Carlsberg in 2006 spoofed the sort of wildlife wall charts that are often given away with newspapers. Although the titles and annotations of the charts were about fish, animals and birds, the pictures showed them in the food form. The endline was, 'Probably the best wall chart in the world'.

01 / Carslberg
This Carlsberg insert is annotated like a wildlife wall chart, but the visuals show the animals in edible form.

02 / Adidas
This Adidas ad annotates a photograph to show how runners see the world. It's an insight that the target audience would find credible.

03 / Penguin
Annotating pictures with numbers to promote words is a surprising choice in this Malaysian campaign for Penguin Books.

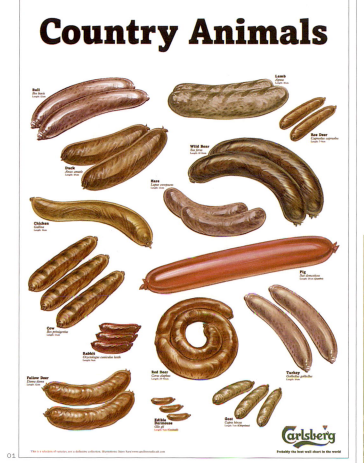

01

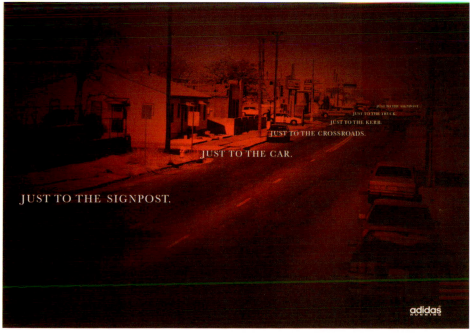

02

03

Switching to an unusual angle can produce intriguing visuals.

81

PERSPECTIVE CHANGE

01

Messing around with perspective can create interesting visual effects. Many ads show familiar things from unusual angles, or present situations from unexpected close-ups or aerial shots.

A campaign for Spuk Stock Pictures recreated famous shots from unfamiliar angles. The Beatles crossing Abbey Road were seen from above, Marylin Monroe in *The Seven Year Itch* was seen from underneath and Muhammad Ali standing over a fallen Sonny Liston was shown from behind. The line was, 'See the unseen', a reference to Spuk's wide offering of stock pictures.

In-depth news investigated from every point of view. CAPE TIMES Know all about it.

01 / Spuk
This campaign for a photo library recreated iconic shots from unusual angles. The endline was 'See the unseen'.

02 / Cape Times
'In-depth news investigated from every angle'. This ad for the *Cape Times* shows the famous 1989 Tiananmen Square protest from inside the tank.

03 / Parmalat
Unusual perspectives can generate humour. This Argentinian ad for fat-free milk uses an overhead view for comic exaggeration.

The *Cape Times* used the same technique in a campaign with the line, 'In-depth news investigated from every angle'. Executions included the Tiananmen Square protester viewed from inside the tank and the Moon landing viewed from inside the lunar module.

Unusual perspectives can also generate humour. An Argentinian ad for Parmalat light milk shows a rainy street scene from above. Most people are using umbrellas, but the Parmalat drinker can shelter beneath her handbag. The unusual angle allows for a clever comic exaggeration.

A campaign for No Bugs fly spray by Grey Auckland showed the product through the honeycomb perspective of a fly. The line was, 'The last thing a fly ever sees'.

Leche Parmalat light. 0% de grasa. ✳ parmalat

82

DETAILS

01 / VW
'The only squeaks and rattles you'll ever hear in a Volkswagen'. Making the baby a detail in a wider product shot gives this layout more humour.

02 / Band Sports
Family portraits might seem a non-sequitur for Brazilian network Band Sports. But the detail of the father's eyes makes it obvious what's going on.

03 / PSP
At first the man seems to be handcuffed to the lamp-post, but closer inspection reveals that he's actually engrossed in the PSP.

Some ads bury their central idea as a detail in a wide shot. It can be a risky strategy, especially on outdoor sites, but it can work if the detail is rewarding enough.

A Spanish ad for the PlayStation Portable showed what appeared to be a man handcuffed to a lamp-post by a policeman. However, a closer look reveals that it's the games console itself that's keeping him immobile. It's a clever exaggeration of gaming addiction.

Brazilian TV network Band Sports ran a series of ads that seemed to be regular family portraits. Closer inspection reveals that the eyes of the father in each case are looking to the side, presumably at an out-of-sight TV. A fresh take on the old idea of putting the product above all else.

Consigning an important element to a detail of a wider shot can also be an art direction choice. An ad for the VW Golf showed the head of a baby peeping out of the back window of the car, alongside the line, 'The only squeaks and rattles you'll ever hear in a Volkswagen'. Making the baby the main visual element might have seemed the obvious choice, but using it as a detail in a product shot gave the ad humour and charm.

The only squeaks and rattles you'll ever hear in a Volkswagen.

Who objects to decibels of delight coming from the back of their car?

Or to being able to actually hear a conversation, or the radio?

What is objectionable, is listening to the irritating results of shoddy workmanship and lazy engineering.

Which is why we at Volkswagen are so dedicated to building the soundest cars on the road.

To Volkswagen, silence isn't golden, it's dull grey, high tensile steel that we form into a rigid safety cell.

Inside, underneath, and around that rigid cell our engineers, robots and computers quietly set to work.

We make sure 10,000 times over, that a door shuts with a reassuring thud, not a hollow slam.

We torture bodywork.

We torment axles and wheel mountings.

And if something squeals in less than 300 hours of merciless testing, we dispose of it.

Why go to such great lengths?

Because there's something that's very important you ought to know when you buy a family car.

That it's a lot more than just sound.

Golf VW

01

02

03

83

THE EFFECTS OF TIME

01 / New Zealand Road Safety
A life would flash before your eyes if you sped past the images in this New Zealand road safety campaign.

02 / Sony
This ad for a Sony TV showed someone's life passing in a series of jump cuts. Many ads use the idea of the product outliving the consumer.

Playing with the effects of time can produce interesting executions. The most obvious examples are ads that assert the durability of a product by showing it surviving into the future or outliving the people who bought it. An eighties ad for Sony's Trinitron TV showed a man on a sofa watching it from birth to death, with his life passing in jump cuts.

Playing with time can also be used to tackle subtler messages. A British campaign for Oxfam's second-hand charity shops showed vintage copies of *Vogue* magazine with the line 'Now in'. A campaign for Greenpeace described the extinction of whales from a future perspective. It gave a novel take on a familiar problem.

The notion that your life flashes in front of your eyes before you die has been used in many ads, and one of the most inventive spins on it came from a road safety campaign by Saatchi & Saatchi New Zealand. Billboards showing scenes from a man's life were placed closely together at the side of the road so that anyone speeding past would see them as a blur of images. The final posters read, 'Don't let your life flash before you' and 'Slow down'.

01

02

84

DRAMATIZING THE NEGATIVE

01/123fleurs
This Grey Paris campaign for 123fleurs. com showed over-the-top consequences of choosing the wrong surprise gifts.

02/Oxy
This campaign for spot treatment Oxy showed us the perspective of people too ashamed to look up.

03/Talon
The classic way of dramatizing the negative is to show the awful consequences of using an inferior product, as in this Talon zipper ad.

Ads that dramatize the negative show what happens if you don't use the product. Such ads can often feel pretty basic, but they can work well if the consequences are surprising enough.

A vintage campaign for Talon zippers shows the classic format of dramatizing the negative. The ads show people who've used inferior zips, with embarrassing results. A man is seen covering his fly with his briefcase above the line 'A prominent New York stockbroker just went public'. An ad about a woman's dress zipper failing on a night at the theatre has the headline 'Last night Mrs Mary Powers opened on Broadway'.

A campaign for a flower-delivery service by Grey Paris showed the awful consequences of other birthday surprises. One ad showed two skywriting planes that have crashed while tracing out the shape of a love heart in the sky. Another showed a woman who's suffered a heart attack after seeing a jack-in-the-box with a 'Happy Birthday' banner.

A campaign for Oxy face wash by Ogilvy & Mather Singapore showed point-of-view shots of shoes and sandals with the line 'Face the world'. The consequences of not using the spot treatment are so obvious they can be implied rather than shown.

01

FACE THE WORLD

02

A prominent New York stockbroker just went public.

It's bad enough when the market takes a sudden plunge. But when your trouser ripper goes down, you lose another kind of security. So for your own good, look for the Talon *Zephyr* nylon zipper next time you buy yourself a suit or a pair of slacks. The *Zephyr* zipper is designed not to snag, or jam. And a little device called *Memory Lock* will make sure your zipper stays up. So all you'll have to worry about going down are your stocks.

03

85

Some ads give a surreal or exaggerated take on the experience of using a product.

DRAMATIZING PRODUCT EXPERIENCE

01 / Coco de Mer
No prizes for guessing what sort of experience this campaign for British sex shop Coco de Mer was trying to dramatize.

02 / Metz
The 'judder' you experience upon sipping the alcopop Metz was depicted as creepy and surreal in this classic campaign.

03 / Tango
'You know when you've been Tango'd'. Many drinks ads attempt to depict what it feels like to sip the drink.

Many ads attempt to dramatize the experience of using the product. In its most basic form, this method shows someone sampling the product, followed by a visual metaphor for their experience.

Lots of drink ads attempt to show us what it's like to take a sip. This can involve a clichéd depiction of refreshment using water or ice. Tango introduced a welcome note of surrealism to this convention with their 'You know when you've been Tango'd' campaign in the early nineties. The most famous execution featured an orange man sneaking up on someone and slapping them on both cheeks at once to show 'the real orange hit of Tango'. It was voted one of the top five British TV ads of all time in a 2000 poll.

The same agency, HHCL, created an even stranger depiction of the product experience for the alcopop Metz. The campaign was based around the 'judder' you feel when sipping it. The infamous 'Judderman' execution showed a man turning into an eerie puppet as he drank it.

An ambitious campaign for British sex shop Coco de Mer attempted to convey the experience of orgasm using surreal bursts of colour. The executions were titled, 'Oooh', 'Ungh', 'Yeeah' and 'Aaagh'.

01

02

03

86

Playing with scale can be an effective way of creating visuals. Countless ads show giant people stomping around cities, or huge products descending from the sky.

SCALE

01/ **Weru**
Altering scale can be used to communicate a range of propositions. In this ad for Weru soundproof windows, smaller objects stand for reduced noise.

02/ **KFC**
Big Ad. Sometimes the scale of the ad itself is the idea. This KFC logo in the Nevada desert was large enough to be seen on Google Earth.

03/ **Quality Street**
Playing with scale can produce entertaining visuals. This poster used humorous exaggeration to launch larger Quality Street chocolates.

This technique is often used when the proposition is to do with size. When Nestlé launched larger versions of their Quality Street chocolates in the UK, posters showed wrappers large enough to obstruct trains and cover faces. It was a classic comic exaggeration of a product feature.

Differences in scale can also communicate more lateral propositions. A German ad for Weru soundproof windows showed noisy things such as fire engines, jets, lawnmowers and bottle banks shrunk down to small sizes. Adding a neat visual gag, the people using these objects stayed normal size.

Lots of ambient ads and special builds play with the scale of the ad itself. A poster campaign for Germany's Görtz stores ran small billboards showing children's shoes next to full-size billboards showing adult ones.

A miniature village in Antwerp also ran small billboards, adding tiny remote-control advertising trucks to their campaign. To promote *Austin Powers: The Spy Who Shagged Me*, tiny billboards showing Mini Me were constructed next to full-size ones showing Austin Powers.

At the other end of the scale, several brands have laid claim to the world's biggest ad. The most audacious might have been the 2007 KFC logo built in the Nevada desert. Consisting of 65,000 tiles covering 87,500 square feet, the construction seems very expensive and elaborate for such a remote location. Or at least it did until you realized that the brand was actually constructing a logo big enough to be seen on Google Earth.

01

02

03

87

*Some campaigns link a product
to positive national stereotypes.*

NATIONAL IDENTITY

01 / Molson
This ad for Molson beer attempted to stir up national pride in Canadians with references to hockey, woolly hats and beavers.

02 / Ikea
Ikea's 'Stop being so English' campaign urged the nation to lose its uptight pretensions.

03 / Fosters
Fosters and XXXX have both based long-running campaigns around laidback Aussie stereotypes.

Products are sometimes linked to their countries of origin. This can be to associate a brand with positive national stereotypes, or to stir up national pride. It's an especially common tactic in alcohol advertising, which is often subject to strict regulations that limit other product claims.

Plenty of lager brands exploit the characteristics associated with their countries. In the UK, both Fosters and XXXX were keen to link themselves with easygoing Australian stereotypes. Fosters used the line 'Drink Australian, think Australian', while their rivals used 'Australians wouldn't give a XXXX for anything else'. Both led to entertaining, if rather interchangeable, executions.

Molson's 'I am Canadian' ad attempted to stir up national pride. It took the form of a rousing speech that celebrated the differences between Canadians and their neighbours to the south. It became a viral hit with ex-pat Canadians around the world via video-sharing sites.

A more surprising take on national stereotypes came from Ikea's 'Stop being so English' campaign. It featured a blond Swedish man criticizing the English for their 'sad and ridiculous' class system. He urges them to drop their pretentions to upper-class respectability and buy furniture that's more relaxed and less formal.

01

02

Foster's. The Australian for lager.

03

88

Characteristics associated with certain regions can be attributed to products.

REGIONAL IDENTITY

01 / Boddingtons
'By 'eck! You smell gorgeous tonight, petal.' This Boddingtons ad used regional dialogue to enjoyably bathetic effect.

02 / Harvey Nichols
When Harvey Nichols opened a store in Bristol, they used Aardman Animations' characters Wallace and Gromit in their ads.

03 / Sunkist
'Everybody knows the best nuts come from California'. These Sunkist ads poked fun at eccentric West Coast stereotypes.

As well as national identity, campaigns can also be based around the specific region a product comes from.

In the UK, the TV work for the Boddingtons 'Cream of Manchester' campaign featured people in glamorous locations speaking in the down-to-earth tone associated with the city. In the US, a campaign for Sunkist nuts showed a psychic healer, a woman channelling spirits and a man who thought he'd been abducted by aliens. The line was, 'Everybody knows the best nuts come from California'.

In 2008, the department store Harvey Nichols opened a store in Bristol, the city that's home to Aardman Animations. DDB's ads to announce the opening featured Aardman's most famous characters, Wallace and Gromit, modelling fashions from the store. It was a great use of regional associations to create a comic juxtaposition.

Chrysler's 2011 Super Bowl ad was a more serious take on regional identity. To a backing of Eminem's 'Lose Yourself', the Chrysler is shown driving through bleak scenes of modern Detroit. A voiceover declares, 'We're from America, but this isn't New York, nor the windy city, or sin city. And we're certainly no one's emerald city.' Acknowledging manufacturing decline and recession was surprising in a Super Bowl spot, and it gave the ad a sombre sense of credibility.

01

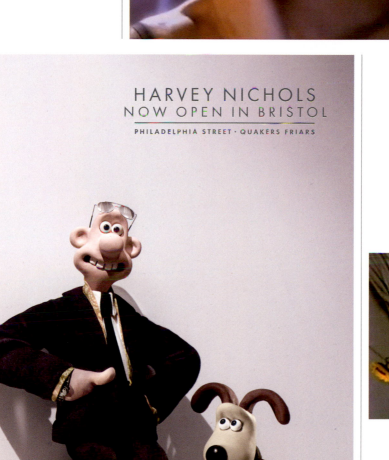

HARVEY NICHOLS
NOW OPEN IN BRISTOL

PHILADELPHIA STREET · QUAKERS FRIARS

03

89

ALTERNATIVE USES

01/Rute 180
This ad for Danish clothes shop Rute 180 shows a man blowing his nose on a T-shirt and throwing it in the bin. The line is, 'T-shirt is only Dkr 99 anyway'.

02/Evian
This campaign for Evian showed people bathing in the water, using it in a goldfish bowl and even freezing it to make an igloo.

03/Araldite
This Araldite glue ad was one of the first special builds to gain coverage in the national press.

A simple way to communicate a benefit can be to find a surprising new use for a product. For example, an ad for extra-strong condoms showed a wrist tied to a bedpost with one.

A famous special build for Araldite glue in the early eighties stuck a yellow Ford Cortina to a billboard along with the line 'It also sticks handles to teapots'. A follow-up added a red Cortina to the yellow one and changed the line to 'The tension mounts'. Finally, the car was removed, leaving a large hole in the billboard, and the line was changed to 'How did we pull it off?'

Danish store Rute 180 demonstrated how cheap its clothes were by showing people putting them to other uses. In one execution, a man blows his nose on a T-shirt and then throws it in the bin. In another, a woman gives an Alsatian a trainer to chew on so it will stop barking.

Evian's 'L'original' campaign showed a series of stylized images of people putting bottled water to odd uses. A woman bathed in it, a barman served it in a cocktail glass and another woman emptied out a bottle into a goldfish bowl. A second burst of posters took the campaign into surreal territory, with an Eskimo freezing Evian to make an igloo and an angel making an Evian cloud.

01

L'original

02

It also sticks handles to teapots.

03

90

TRANSFORMATION

Some ads show how a product can transform the world or the way we see it.

A spoof Duff Beer ad in *The Simpsons* showed a group of protesting feminists getting sprayed with lager and turning into bikini-clad models. As well as satirizing sexist beer ads, it also sent up transformation in advertising.

Showing a product transforming people or environments can come across as patronizing and contrived. But the technique can work if done in a humorous or original way.

A Brazilian campaign showed men transforming from ugly to attractive, bald to thick-haired and fat to ripped as boxes of jewellery were opened. It's a simple visual joke that rings sadly true.

A good variation on transformation can be to show things becoming weirder rather than more idyllic. A campaign for Smirnoff vodka turned a bottle into a lens that showed a darker and more mysterious world. Sheep became wolves, surgeons became cannibals, goldfish became piranhas and angels became Hell's Angels.

Another variation uses captions to imply transformation without actually showing it. A campaign for the sportswear brand Umbro showed everyday scenes such as lamp-posts, shelters, trees, gates and fences with the line 'Approved goal'. To the sports-mad youngster, everywhere becomes a potential playing field.

01 / Comfort
Showing the world before and after using the product is a pretty basic technique but it can work well with entertaining visuals such as these.

02 / Umbro
Transformation can be implied as well as shown. Umbro's 'Approved goal' campaign showed how the whole world can be a playing field for the sports fan.

03 / Smirnoff
The product doesn't always have to transform things for the better. The world seen through the bottle in this classic Smirnoff campaign was weirder and darker.

DON'T ROUGH IT.   LIVE LIFE IN COMFORT.

01

02

03

91

*Products can be transformed
to produce inventive visual
metaphors or visual similes.*

PRODUCT TRANSFORMATION

01 / Fisherman's Friend
This campaign for the strong lozenges Fisherman's Friend used origami to transform the packet into fearsome shapes.

02 / Boddingtons
The 'Cream of Manchester' campaign for Boddingtons Bitter turned the product into different objects associated with cream.

03 / Guinness Extra Cold
The famous black-and-white pint was transformed into things such as ice lollies and fans in this campaign of visual similes.

Rather than showing people or environments transforming, some ads show the product itself transforming.

Product transformations usually manipulate a product shot into a visual metaphor, simile or pun. A campaign for the strong menthol lozenges Fisherman's Friend showed the packet folded into the shapes of a shark, rhino and T-Rex. The line was, 'Be warned'.

A campaign for Guinness Extra Cold turned the black-and-white pint into an ice lolly, fan, erect nipple and iceberg. The similes were rendered in a simple graphic style.

A famous campaign for Boddingtons used the line 'The cream of Manchester' and transformed the pint glass into things associated with cream. Initial executions turned the product into ice creams and cream cakes, and the campaign developed into visual puns on the phrases 'whipped cream', 'hand cream' and 'cream tea'.

Product transformation can also work on TV. A 2006 ad showed a Citroën C4 turning into a robot in the style of the Transformers franchise and dancing around a car park. The line was, 'Alive with technology'. The ad became an online hit, and spawned follow-ups in which the car went ice skating, ran down a winding road and strutted around New York to a cover version of 'Stayin' Alive'.

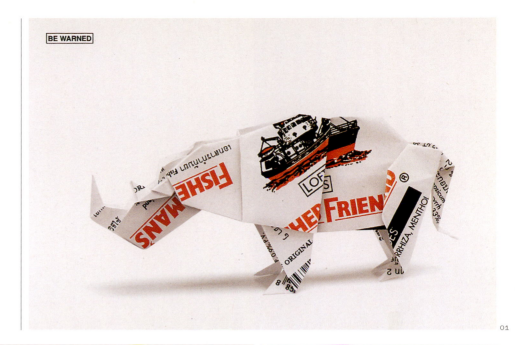

BE WARNED

01

BODDINGTONS. THE CREAM OF MANCHESTER.

Boddingtons Draught Bitter. Brewed at the Strangeways Brewery since 1778.

02

NEW GUINNESS EXTRA COLD

03

Campaigns can focus on the
history of a company or brand.

92

HERITAGE

Brands that have long and interesting histories often base campaigns around their heritage, sometimes using deliberately outdated language and art direction to evoke authenticity.

One of the most famous heritage campaigns in the UK is for Hovis bread. 'Boy on a Bike', a 1973 ad directed by Ridley Scott, showed a delivery boy pushing a bike up a steep northern street to Dvorak's 'New World' Symphony. It was voted Britain's favourite TV ad in a poll in 2006.

Jack Daniels also has a long-running heritage campaign. Black-and-white images of workers in the Tennessee distillery are placed above headlines or chunks of copy detailing the care that goes into making the whisky.

Sometimes brands can use their heritage to exploit recurring fashions. A revival of fifties fashions in the eighties allowed brands such as Levi's and Brylcreem to exploit their associations with the era. A Levi's ad featuring a man stripping down to his underwear in a launderette managed to boost sales not just of the jeans, but also of the boxer shorts he was wearing underneath.

Nostalgic advertising also tends to become more popular in times of economic recession, when people feel uncertain about the future. After the 2008 crash, some brands even re-ran vintage ads, at once asserting their heritage and saving on production costs.

There Are Times At Jack Daniel's When
You Can't Do Anything But Sit
And Wait. So That's Exactly What We Do.

You see, every drop of Jack Daniel's is seeped for days through twelve-foot vats of finely packed charcoal. Called charcoal mellowing, this time-taking Tennessee process is the old, natural way of smoothing out whiskey...and there's nothing a man can do to speed it along.

After a sip of Jack Daniel's, we believe, you'll be glad the folks in our hollow are content to do nothing when that's what's called for.

SMOOTH SIPPIN' TENNESSEE WHISKEY

If you'd like to know more about our unique whiskey, write to us for a free booklet at the Jack Daniel's Distillery, Lynchburg, Tennessee, USA.

01

01 / **Jack Daniels**
Jack Daniels advertising is in many ways the definitive heritage campaign. Headlines and copy detail the 'old-time traditions' of the distillery.

02 / **Levi's**
Fashion revivals can inspire heritage advertising. This Levi's campaign ran when fifties styles were back in vogue.

03 / **Hovis**
'It's as good for you today as it's always been'. This heritage ad for Hovis bread was directed by Ridley Scott.

02

03

93

PRODUCT STORY

01 / Coke
Product-story ads can also imagine fantastical processes of manufacturing, as in Coke's 'Happiness Factory' spot.

02 / Le Creuset
This campaign for cookware makers Le Creuset described the manufacturing process in the language of cookery books.

03 / Parker
Long-copy ads detailing manufacturing processes were once common. Even if you didn't read the copy, they gave the impression of quality and craftsmanship.

As well as focusing on a brand's history, ads can also detail a product's manufacturing process. This can be a straight account of the care that goes into making something, or a fantastical reimagining of the process.

Descriptions of the meticulous ways products are made were a common feature of long-copy press ads, such as the pen ad that read, 'Hopefully the Parker Cirrus will last a lifetime. It took long enough to make.' It didn't really matter if you read the copy or not. The mere presence of large blocks of text describing manufacturing processes was enough to signify quality.

Other ads condense product stories into headlines, such as the campaign for Le Creuset that laid out the ingredients of the cookware as a recipe.

Another type of product-story ad invents an imaginary manufacturing process. Coke's 'Happiness Factory' ad showed computer-generated characters producing the drink in a series of colourful landscapes. An ad for Australian beer Hahn SuperDry showed it being filtered through speakers, drum kits and stacks of sporting trophies, and then stored in a vat covered in a huge rhinestone suit, with the *Knight Rider* theme playing throughout. The line was, 'Super goes in. SuperDry taste comes out.'

01

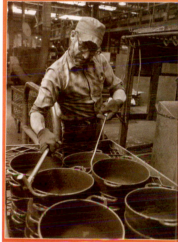

CASSEROLE PROVENCALE:

8 lbs Pig Iron,
2 lbs Sand,
2 lbs Coke,
1 lb Enamel.

Cook in factory for 30 mins at 800°C (or Gas Mark 24). Glaze, then enamel. Re-heat. Leave for three days. Serve.

© LE CREUSET

02

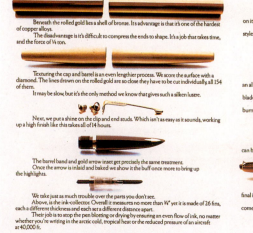

Hopefully a Parker Cirrus will last a lifetime. It takes long enough to make.

Beneath the rolled gold lies a shell of bronze. It's advantage is that it's one of the hardest of copper alloys.

The disadvantage is it's difficult to compress the ends to shape. It's a job that takes time, and the force of ¼ ton.

Texturing the cap and barrel is an even lengthier process. We score the surface with a diamond. The lines drawn on the rolled gold are so close they have to be cut individually, all 154 of them.

It may be slow, but it's the only method we know that gives such a silken lustre.

Next, we put a shine on the clip and end studs. Which isn't as easy as it sounds, working up a high finish like this takes all of 14 hours.

The barrel band and gold arrow inset get precisely the same treatment.

Once the arrow is inlaid and baked we show it the buff once more to bring up the highlights.

We take just as much trouble over the parts you don't see.

Above, is the ink-collector. Overall it measures no more than ¾" yet it is made of 26 fins, each a different thickness and each set a different distance apart.

Their job is to stop the pen blotting or drying by ensuring an even flow of ink, no matter whether you're writing in the arctic cold, tropical heat or the reduced pressure of an aircraft at 40,000 ft.

The nib is of 14 carat gold, and although it may be the smallest part, more time is spent on it than any other.

It takes no fewer than 15 operations to turn the blank, above, into one of the eight nib styles below.

Extra fine. Fine. Fine oblique. Medium. Medium oblique. Broad. Broad oblique. Stub.

After being stamped, trimmed and worked into shape, the nib's tipped with ruthenium, an alloy four times harder than steel and ten times as smooth.

Then the most delicate task; splitting the nib to conduct the ink. It's cut by hand, with a blade no thicker than a human hair.

More polishing follows, 18 hours this time. Unfortunately, there are no short cuts when burnishing gold.

Apart from the shell, there's an inner tube of stainless steel to protect the ink-sac (which can be replaced with a cartridge of Quink simply by unscrewing it).

At long last, the finished pen. It has been filled, written with, cleaned and given a final inspection.

While we know that nothing in this world can ever be perfect, we feel the Parker Cirrus comes very, very close.

φ PARKER

THE PARKER CIRRUS COSTS £18. THERE IS ALSO A MATCHING CIRRUS BALL PEN AND PENCIL, £9 EACH. RECOMMENDED RETAIL PRICES INCLUDING VAT.

03

Focusing on a single feature of a product can demonstrate its overall quality.

94

PRODUCT FEATURES

While some ads describe the process of making a product, others attempt to imply quality by focusing on a single feature. Such ads might result from a planner or creative unearthing a fact that speaks volumes about a product's overall quality.

The most famous product-detail ad is probably David Ogilvy's 1958 Rolls-Royce execution: 'At 60 miles an hour the loudest noise in this new Rolls-Royce comes from the electric clock'. In his classic book *Ogilvy on Advertising*, he claims to have come up with the line after three weeks of research. In these days of separate creative and planning departments, it's difficult to imagine a copywriter being allowed three weeks to unearth a similar gem now. But recognizing when a product feature is interesting enough to become the ad is still an important skill.

A British campaign for Heinz that ran in the nineties used a series of facts that implied quality. They included 'While others use starch to thicken their tomato ketchup, Heinz just use tomatoes', and 'If it comes out faster than 0.028 mph, we reject it'.

The 'Homemade Ltd' campaign for Ben and Jerry's picked out a number of features that showed the ice cream retained a hand-crafted quality. One of the executions was, 'We thought about buying some scales to measure out the pecans. Then we thought let's just buy more pecans.'

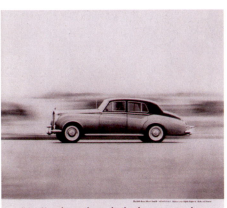

01

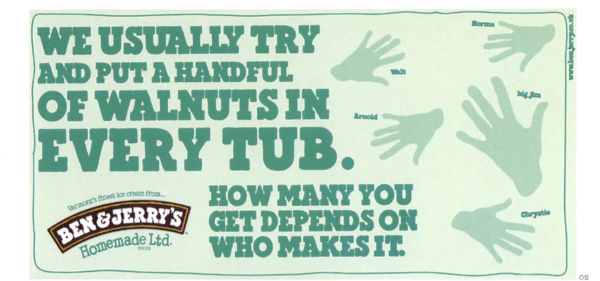

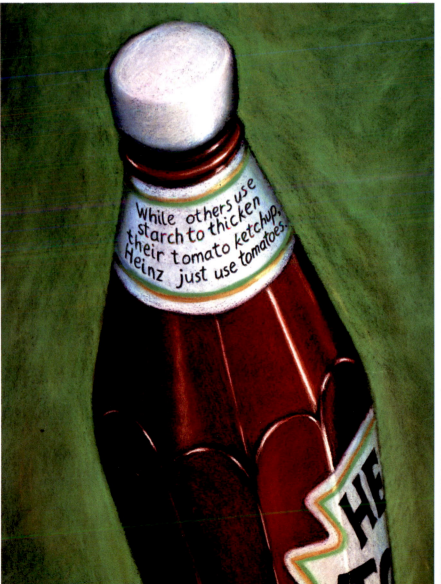

01 / Rolls-Royce
This vintage Rolls-Royce ad is still the definitive product-feature ad. A small detail about the car implies its overall quality.

02 / Ben and Jerry's
This campaign for Ben and Jerry's ice cream uncovered product details that emphasized the homemade feel of the global brand.

03 / Heinz
This ad was part of a campaign that picked out telling features about a variety of Heinz products.

95

LOCAL KNOWLEDGE

01 / 'Tate Gallery by Tube'
This poster used the double meaning of the word 'tube' to create an arty update of Harry Beck's classic map design.

02 / LTDA
Outdoor ads can refer to their local surroundings. This ad for London black cabs poked fun at rival minicabs.

03 / Decode Jay-Z
This Bing campaign used clues on Twitter and Facebook to direct fans to the locations of pages from Jay-Z's autobiography, *Decoded*.

As well as researching a product, it's also worth researching the place an ad is running. Many outdoor ads, local newspaper ads and online ads include a knowing reference to the nearby area.

London Transport's 'Tate Gallery by Tube' poster is a good example of using local knowledge to create an in-joke. It plays on a double meaning of the word 'tube', referring both to the paint container and to the London Underground. The ad was so popular it became a bestselling print, and can still be bought today.

Outdoor ads that reference their local surroundings can stand out. A campaign for the Licensed Taxi Drivers Association pointed out some obvious landmarks for the benefit of minicab drivers who lacked local knowledge.

Online and social media have allowed ads to use local knowledge in a much more sophisticated way. Droga5's 'Decode Jay-Z with Bing' campaign for Bing placed pages of Jay-Z's autobiography, *Decoded* in the places that inspired them, using locations from New York to Glastonbury in the UK. Clues on Twitter and Facebook directed fans to each location on Bing Maps, allowing them to assemble the book digitally before its physical release. It was an innovative way of promoting both the book and the search engine.

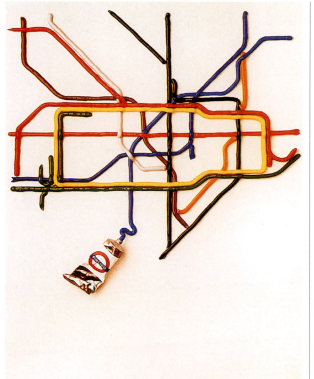

THE TATE GALLERY

01

02

03

Getting a celebrity to endorse a product doesn't have to lead to dull ads.

96

ENDORSEMENT

Celebrity endorsement is an industry in itself now, encompassing public relations, social media and traditional ads. It can sometimes lead to primitive advertising, where the mere presence of a star is assumed to be so exciting there's no need for any other attempt to entertain. But it doesn't have to.

Sportswear brands like Nike and Adidas are famous for the executional brilliance of their celebrity campaigns, and have created classics such as Nike's 'Michael Jordan 1, Isaac Newton 0'.

Picking unusual people can make for surprising endorsement ads. The launch campaign for British TV channel BBC Four featured highbrow figures such as Ian McEwan, Philip Glass and Susan Sontag.

Another interesting approach can be to highlight a genuine endorsement that a celebrity has given unprompted. Barack Obama mentioned in an interview that he read the *Financial Times*. The paper turned the quote into a press ad, creating what must be one of the highest-profile endorsements ever.

As with reverse testimonials, reverse endorsements ironically twist advertising conventions by featuring celebrities telling you not to use the product.

An Australian campaign for Virgin Mobile was based around the conceit that eighties teen idol Jason Donovan's phone number had been leaked by the press and he wanted people to stop prank-calling him. The brand ran ads urging the public to use their 'excessively low rates' responsibly. Of course the whole thing was a hoax that Donovan was in on, but the price message was communicated in an original way.

01

MICHAEL JORDAN 1
ISAAC NEWTON 0

If he can make it, so can Volkswagen.

No disrespect intended, Mr. Feldman. But no-one would ever mistake you for Gregory Peck. Yet you've made it right to the top.
On talent.
And that's kind of reassuring when you make a car that looks like ours.
The Volkswagen isn't pretty, Mr. Feldman. But it's got talent.
It has an air-cooled engine that can't boil over in the summer.
Or freeze up in the winter.
It's the kind of engine that can go on and on and on.
We know one person who went right on for 248,000 miles.
And for a little car its got a great talent for fitting people in.
There's more headroom than you'd expect. (Over 37½" from seat to roof.)
If you were 6' 7" Mr. Feldman you still wouldn't hit the roof.
And because there's no engine in the front, there's room to stretch your legs in the front.
We've even got a space behind the back seat where you can sleep a baby. In a carrycot.
So you see, Mr. Feldman, looks aren't everything are they?

01 / Virgin Mobile
Reverse endorsement. Virgin Mobile's plea for customers to stop calling Jason Donovan's phone highlighted their cheap rates.

02 / Nike
Celebrity endorsement doesn't have to lead to bland executions. Lots of classic ads like this Nike poster have featured celebrities.

03 / VW
An unusual celebrity choice can create a surprising endorsement campaign. This ground-breaking VW ad featured odd-looking comic Marty Feldman.

97

TESTIMONIAL

01 / Electricity Board
Nick Park animated genuine vox pops in this campaign for the British Electricity Board. It made for an engaging spin on the testimonial format.

02 / VW
In this classic VW ad, an elderly couple from Missouri describe how they replaced their mule with a Beetle. Testimonials from unusual or unexpected customers can be an entertaining twist.

03 / El Al
Rather than going for a straight 'staff testimonial' by getting a pilot to talk about the airline, this El Al ad gave the perspective of a pilot's mother.

Testimonials were once a dominant form of advertising, but most consumers are pretty sceptical about them now.

However, an executional twist can make the format engaging. A British campaign for the Electricity Board accompanied the voices of satisfied customers with cute animation of animals by Nick Park. The technique of mixing documentary audio and stylized visuals has been imitated a lot since.

Another common twist on testimonial advertising is to pick out people who give an unusual perspective on a product, such as the classic VW press ad featuring a Midwestern couple who'd replaced their mule with a Beetle. Another famous example is the El Al ad written from the perspective of a pilot's mother. Channelling product messages through parental pride made for a fresh and colloquial tone of voice.

Customer testimonials have become very important in the age of online reviews. Feedback and star ratings on sites such as Amazon and Trip Advisor can make a huge difference to the success of products and services. But has the process become another branch of advertising? Studies have found that many online testimonials are in fact the products of 'opinion spammers' who are paid to write glowing five-star reviews.

01

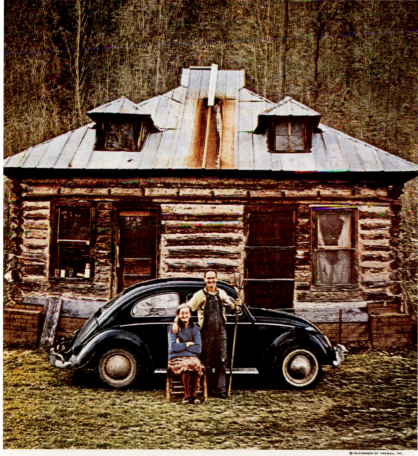

© VOLKSWAGEN OF AMERICA, INC.

"It was the only thing to do after the mule died."

Three years back, the Hinsleys of Dora, Missouri, had a tough decision to make.

To buy a new mule.

Or invest in a used bug.

They weighed the two possibilities.

First there was the problem of the bitter Ozark winters. Tough on a warm-blooded mule. Not so tough on an air-cooled VW.

Then, what about the eating habits of the two contenders? Hay vs. gasoline.

As Mr. Hinsley puts it: "I get over eighty miles out of a dollar's worth of gas and I get where I want to go a lot quicker."

Then there's the road leading to their cabin. Many a mule pulling a wagon and many a conventional automobile has spent many an hour stuck in the mud.

As for shelter, a mule needs a barn. A bug doesn't. "It just sets out there all day and the paint job looks near as good as the day we got it."

Finally, there was maintenance to think about. When a mule breaks down, there's only one thing to do: Shoot it.

But if and when their bug breaks down, the Hinsleys have a Volkswagen dealer only two gallons away.

02

My son, the pilot.

by Tillie Katz

03

98

REVERSE TESTIMONIAL

In a reverse testimonial, a product is criticized by someone untrustworthy.

As consumers became wise to traditional testimonials, variations on the format were developed. One of the most common was the reverse testimonial, in which the product is criticized by an untrustworthy source.

A wonderfully economical early example was 'I quit school when I were sixteen', a poster promoting high school education in the US. A similar execution was created for *The Economist*'s 'White out of red' poster campaign. The quotation 'I never read The Economist' was attributed to 'Management trainee. Aged 42'. It became one of the best-loved posters of all time, although that didn't stop budget airline EasyJet recycling it virtually word for word in 2003 (although they changed the age of the management trainee to 47).

The 'culture jamming' activities of anti-consumerist groups sometimes use reverse testimonial. Some activists alter the words on existing posters to reveal the truth about big, bad corporations. For example, an athlete's praise for a sportswear brand might be altered to tell the truth about sweatshops, or a celebrity endorsement of a soft drink might be changed to reveal its health risks.

It's a technique that agencies themselves have used too, as in the poster for the California Department of Health Services that posed as a Marlboro ad but highlighted the risks of smoking.

"I never read The Economist."

Management trainee. Aged 42.

01

01 / The Economist
This reverse testimonial from an unnamed management trainee was voted one of the best posters of the century in *Campaign* magazine.

02 / School
Reverse testimonials show the product being criticized by an untrustworthy source. The grammatical mistakes undermine the statement in this further-education ad.

03 / California Department of Health Services
The 'culture-jamming' activities of anti-consumerist groups were eventually adopted by ad agencies themselves, as in this Marlboro pastiche.

"I quit school when I were sixteen."

02

Bob, I've got emphysema.

California Department Of Health Services.
Funded By The Tobacco Tax Initiative.

03

99

MANUFACTURER'S TESTIMONIAL

01/47.3 Perdue
'It takes a tough man to make a tender chicken'. Company owners and founders regularly appeared in their own advertising in the sixties, seventies and eighties.

02/Outpost.com
By the late nineties, the manufacturer's testimonial had become a staple of the spoof, as in these humorously cruel ads for Outpost.com.

03/Tango
Tango's celebrated 'St George' ad begins as a low-key manufacturer's testimonial and builds into a widescreen epic, blending two extremes of advertising.

Another variation on the testimonial is one that's delivered by the founder or owner of a company.

Showing the CEO on the factory floor or demonstrating the product was a staple of hard-sell advertising in the sixties, seventies and eighties. Lee Iacocca of Chrysler showed off various models and advised, 'If you can find a better car, buy it.' Dave Thomas of Wendy's tried his own burgers and said, 'Gee, this is pretty good'. Colonel Sanders was served 'Finger lickin' good' Kentucky Fried Chicken in his own restaurants. And Frank Perdue explained that 'It takes a tough man to make a tender chicken.'

By the late nineties, the genre had become the preserve of cheap local car-dealership ads and spoofs. Cliff Freeman's Outpost.com campaign featured a genial-looking CEO sitting in a leather armchair introducing his efforts to get you to remember the company name. They included releasing a pack of wolves on a marching band and firing gerbils out of a cannon.

In Britain, Tango's 'St George' ad began with what appeared to be a genuine spokesperson for the brand responding to the complaints of a French exchange student. Over the course of 90 seconds, the ad morphs from a mundane spot in the 4:3 aspect ratio to a widescreen, effects-laden epic. It makes for a hilarious shift of tone.

01

02

03

100

STAFF

Showing the dedication of a company's staff is a good way to imply the quality of its products

Featuring staff in ads is another traditional type of testimonial. It can give brands a touch of authenticity to show the hard-working people that make up the company. While these kinds of genuine staff endorsements might seem cheesy to modern consumers, variations on the staff campaign live on.

A popular strategy is to portray staff as excessively diligent and dedicated. A campaign for the VW Passat featured the endline 'A car born of obsession'. One of the executions riffed on an old joke by having a woman approach a VW engineer in a bar and ask, 'Is that a ruler in your pocket or are you just pleased to see me?' The engineer takes a ruler out of his pocket and shrugs.

The idea that staff are given rigorous military-style training has also been used. An ad for Little Caesar's pizzas showed a secret training base in the middle of the Gobi Desert where staff are trained in the art of speedy delivery.

The rise of social media has led to some interesting staff campaigns. Best Buy launched their 'Twelpforce' campaign by showing a man asking a question to a stadium full of blue-shirted staff. It was a physical representation of an online service where customers could ask their staff questions on Twitter. The campaign combined TV advertising, social media and online customer service in a modern reinvention of the staff ad.

01 / VW
01 / VW
Many campaigns portray a company's staff as especially dedicated. This VW Passat campaign positioned it as a 'car born of obsession'.

02 / Little Caesars
This Little Caesars ad showed pizza delivery staff undergoing a punishing training regime in the middle of the Gobi Desert.

03 / Twelpforce
Best Buy's 'Twelpforce' campaign offered customers online help from real members of staff. It was a modern take on the staff campaign.

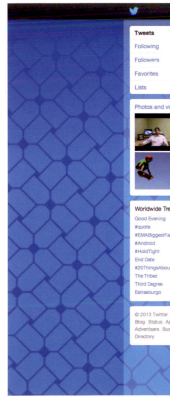

01

02

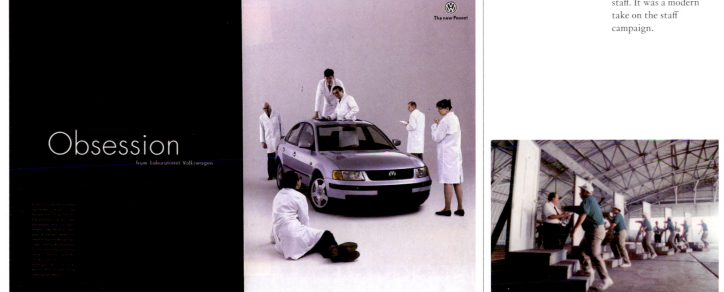

03

INDEX

CREDITS

cover image: Tatiana Koroleva / Alamy /1.1 Agency: Simons Palmer Denton Clemmow & Johnson. Courtesy of The Advertising Archives /1.2 Agency: Wieden+Kennedy Portland /1.3 Reprint courtesy of The Guardian. Agency: Boase Massimi Pollitt /2.1 Courtesy DDB London. Illustrator: Steven Wilson. Richard Branson photo: © Reuters/CORBIS /2.2 Agency: isobel. Art Director: Rob Fletcher. Copywriter: David Alexander. Photographer: Paul Thompson /2.3 Reprint courtesy of The NSPCC. Agency: Saatchi & Saatchi London /3.1 Agency: Lowe Howard-Spink London /3.2 Agency: Saatchi & Saatchi London. Courtesy of The Advertising Archives /3.3 Agency: Saatchi & Saatchi London /4.1 Agency: McCann-Erickson Manchester. Courtesy of The Advertising Archives /4.2 Agency: BBDO London /4.3 Agency: Fallon Minneapolis /5.1 Agency: Collett Dickenson Pearce /5.2 Courtesy of a&eDDB London /5.3 Courtesy of Arnold Furnace, Sydney. Executive Creative Director: Rob Martin Murphy. Art Director: Luke Duggan. Copywriter: Paul Bootlis. Head of Art: Paul Fenton. Retoucher: Electric Art /6.1 Courtesy of The Advertising Archives /6.2 Agency: JWT, Shanghai. Chairman, Asia Pacific Creative Council: Sheungyan Lo. ECD of Northeast Asia and China Chairman: Yang Yeo. CCO of Shanghai office: Elvis Chau. Creative Director: Hattie Cheng. Art Directors: Rojana Chuasakul, Haoxi Lv, Danny Li, Surachai Puthikulangkur. Copywriter: Marc Wang. Animator: Illusion Co., Ltd. Print Production: Joseph Yu, Lulu Zhang, Isaac Xu. Production House: Illusion Co., Ltd. Illustrator: Surachai Puthikulangkura, Supachai U-Rairat (Illusion). Production House Producer: Anotai, Panmongkol, Somsak Pairew (Illusion) /6.3 Agency: Euro RSCG Flagship /7.1 Agency: JWT Manila /7.2 Reprint courtesy of Tate Gallery /7.3 Agency: Leo Burnett /8.1 Agency: DDB /8.2 Reprint courtesy of Campari America. Agency: Angotti, Thomas, Hedge /8.3 Agency: Fallon McElligott Minneapolis /9.1 Agency: DM9 DBB Sao Paulo. / 9.2 Agency: Wieden+Kennedy /9.3 Agency: BMP /10.1 Courtesy of The Advertising Archives /10.2 Courtesy of BBDO Proximity Malaysia /10.3 Agency: BBDO London /11.1 Agency: Lord & Thomas. Courtesy of The Advertising Archives /11.2 Courtesy of The Advertising Archives /11.3 Agency: Young & Rubicam /12.1 Courtesy of The Advertising Archives /12.2 Courtesy of The Advertising Archives /12.3 Agency: Fallon London /13.1 Agency: Goodby Silverstein and Partners San Francisco /13.2 Agency: AMV BBDO /13.3 Agency: TBWA Chiat Day /14.1 Agency: Lowe London /14.2 Agency: Earle Palmer Brown Bethesda /14.3 Agency: AMV BBDO /15.1 Courtesy DLKW Lowe /15.2 Courtesy of The Advertising Archives /15.3 Agency: Vitruvio Leo Burnett Madrid /16.1 Agency: Colman RSCG /16.2 Agency: Marketforce /16.3 Agency: Miles Calcraft, Briginshaw Duffy /17.1 Agency: D'Arcy London /17.2 Agency: Bartle Bogle Hegarty. Courtesy of The Advertising Archives /17.3 Agency: a&eDDB /18.1 Reprint courtesy of Avis. Agency: Cliff Freeman & Partners /18.2 Agency: Ogilvy and Mather Mexico /18.3 Agency: Shop /19.1 Agency: Collett Dickenson Pearce /19.2 Courtesy Grey Worldwide /19.3 Agency: Collett Dickenson Pearce /20.1 Agency: Wieden+Kennedy London /20.2 Courtesy of The Advertising Archives /20.3 Agency: Fallon London /21.1 Agency: DDB New Zealand. Art Director: Gavin Siakimotu. Copywriter: Hywel James. Executive Creative Director: Paul Catmur /21.2 Agency: a&eDDB /21.3 Agency: Collett Dickenson Pearce /22.1 Agency: WCRS /22.2 Agency; Saatchi & Saatchi /22.3; Saatchi & Saatchi /23.1 Agency: Bartle Bogle Hegarty /23.2 Agency; Arnell Group /23.3 Courtesy of Clemenger BBDO Wellington /24.1

Courtesy of Leo Burnett Toronto /24.2 Courtesy of Ogilvy Cape Town /24.3 Agency: BMP Davidson Pearce /25.1 Agency: DDB /25.3 Agency: Saatchi & Saatchi London /26.1 Agency: BBDO Atlanta /26.2 Agency: a&eDDB. Photography by James Day /27.1 Agency: Simons Palmer /27.2 Agency: Leo Burnett Chicago /27.3 Agency: Lowe Howard-Spink /28.1 Agency: Barker and Dobson /28.2 Agency: Naga DDB Malaysia /28.3 Agency: Scali McCabe Sloves. Courtesy of The Advertising Archives /29.1 Reprint courtesy of Carlsberg. Agency: Saatchi and Saatchi. Courtesy of The Advertising Archives /29.2 Agency: SHOP /29.3 Courtesy of The Advertising Archives /30.1 Agency: Ogilvy South Africa. Creative Directors: Chris Gotz, Gordon Ray. Art Director: Michael Lees-Rolf. Copywriter: Kelly Putter. Illustrator: Karen Cronje /30.2 Agency: JWT Mexico /30.3 Agency: Fallon /31.1 Agency: Mother /31.2 Courtesy of The Advertising Archives /31.3 Agency: Collett Dickinson Pearce /32.1 Courtesy of The Viral Factory /32.2 Image supplied by Barnardo's /32.3 © Richard Olivier/CORBIS /33.1 Agency: Leagas Delaney US /33.2 Agency: DDB Chicago /33.3 Courtesy of Full Contact Advertising Boston /34.1 Agency: Miles Calcraft Briginshaw Duffy /34.2 Agency: Fallon /34.3 Agency: Cliff Freeman & Partners /35.1 Reprint courtesy of AB InBev. Agency: Collett Dickenson Pearce /35.2 Agency: Collett Dickenson Pearce. Courtesy of The Advertising Archives /35.3 Agency: The Martin Agency Richmond /36.1 Agency: BMP /36.2 Agency: AMV BBDO /36.3 Courtesy of Droga5 /37.1 Agency: Ammirati & Puris /37.2 Courtesy of TBWA/Hunt/Lascaris Johannesburg /37.3 Created by Cramer Saatchi /38.1 Agency: Ogilvy & Mather /38.2 Agency: DDB /38.3 Agency: Lowe & Partners /39.1 Agency: KesselsKramer. Art Direction: Erik Kessels. Photographer: Johannes Schwartz /39.2 Agency: Carl Ally /39.3 Agency: HHCL. Courtesy of The Advertising Archives /40.1 Agency: Cliff Freeman & Partners /40.2 Agency: CHI & Partners /40.3 Agency: George Patterson & Partners /41.1 Getty Images /41.2 Courtesy of Mother London /41.3 Courtesy of VCCP /42.1 Agency: Leo Burnett /42.2 The Doughboy character courtesy of The Pillsbury Company, LLC /42.3 Agency: Lowe & Partners. Courtesy of The Advertising Archives /43.1 The Nestea name and image is reproduced with the kind permission of Société des Produits Nestlé S.A /43.2 ©Apple Inc. Used with permission. All rights reserved. Apple® and the Apple logo are registered trademark of Apple Inc /43.3 Agency: BBDO London /44.1 © Bettmann, CORBIS /44.2 Director: Charles Stone III. Writers: Chris Fiore and Charles Stone III. Director of Photography: Shane Hurlbut. Editor: Nico Alba (Union Editorial) /44.3 Created by Pubbliregia /45.1 Agency: Allen, Brady & Marsh /45.2 Agency: Lowe, London. Courtesy of The Advertising Archives /45.3 Agency: Papert Koenig Lois /46.1 Agency: Saatchi & Saatchi NY /46.2 Agency: Chemistry, Dublin. Art Direction: Adrian Fitz-Simon. Copy: Emmet Wright /46.3 Courtesy Breast Cancer Awareness and Saatchi and Saatchi Malaysia /47.1 Agency: Lowe Howard Spink /47.2 Agency: Leagas Delany. Courtesy of The Advertising Archives /47.3 Agency: RPA, USA /48.1 Reprint Courtesy of International Business Machines Corporation, © International Business Machines Corporation. Agency: Saatchi and Saatchi /48.2 Agency: Saatchi and Saatchi /48.3 Agency: AMV BBDO /49.1 Agency: Lowe Howard Spink /49.2 Agency: AMV London /50.1 Agency: The Martin Agency /50.2 Reprint courtesy of Anti-Slavery International. Agency: Saatchi and Saatchi London /50.3 Agency: Mad Dogs and Englishmen, New York. Courtesy of The Advertising Archives /51.1 Courtesy of The Advertising Archives /51.2 Agency: Wieden + Kennedy Portland /51.3 Agency: AMV BBDO /52.1 Agency: Benton and Bowles /52.2 Agency: Crispin Porter + Bogusky /52.3 Agency: Collett Dickinson Pearce. Courtesy of The Advertising Archives /53.1 Courtesy of Droga5 /53.2 Agency: Crispin Porter + Bogusky /53.3 Agency: Lew Lara\TBWA, Brazil /54.1 Agency: DDB London /54.2 Agency: This is Real Art /54.3 Agency: Burkitt DDB /55.1 Agency: Bmp DDB London /55.2 Agency: Wasey Campbell-Ewald /56.1 Agency: Goodby, Silverstein & Partners /56.2 Agency: Leo Burnett Toronto /56.3 Courtesy of The Advertising Archives /57.1 Agency: Leo Burnett Johannesburg /57.2 Agency: Dentsu Y&R /57.3 Agency: Kirshembaum and Bond /58.1 © ART+COM /58.2 Courtesy of Mission Media. Campaign by Nokia to promote "Good Things" a feature of Nokia's OVI Maps. Produced by Mission Media Ltd /58.3 Courtesy Human Rights Watch and art director Roy Wisnu. Agency: JWT New York /59.1 Agency: Leo Burnett Chicago /59.2 Agency: DDB Dusseldorf /59.3 AMV BBDO /60.1 Agency: Colenso BBDO New Zealand /60.2 Agency: CumminsNitro Australia /60.3 Getty Images /61.1 Agency: JWT London /61.2 Agency: Marketforce Advertising /61.3 Agency: Leo Burnett London /62.1 Agency: DDB Vancouver /62.2 Produced by THOMAS THOMAS FILMS /62.3 Agency: Digital Kitchen /63.1 Courtesy of Arnold Worldwide Boston /63.2 Agency: Crispin Porter + Bogusky /63.3 Agency: Saatchi & Saatchi London /64.1 Agency: Crispin Porter + Bogusky /64.2 Agency: Publicis Mojo Auckland /64.3 Agency: BBH. Photo by Pedro Alvarez. Courtesy of The Advertising Archives /65.1 Agency: Saatchi and Saatchi /65.2 Agency: AMVBBDO. Courtesy

of The Advertising Archives /65.3 Director: Baz Luhrman /66.1 Courtesy of Space150 /66.2 Courtesy of The Advertising Archives /66.3 Courtesy of Mother /67.1 The 3-Bars logo is a registered trade mark of the Adidas Group, used with permission. Agency: Mccann-Erickson Manchester /67.2 Agency: GGT London. Courtesy of The Advertising Archives /67.3 Courtesy of 4creative /68.1 Agency: DDB Sydney /68.2 Courtesy of TBWA/Hunt/Lascaris /68.3 The KitKat name and image is reproduced with the kind permission of Société des Produits Nestlé S.A. Agency: JWT London /69.1 Agency: Young and Rubicam Kuala Lumpar /69.2 Agency: AMV BBDO. Illustration: Pâté. Art Direction: Pâté. Copywriter: Mike Nicholson /69.3 Courtesy of RKCR/Y&R /70.1 Agency: Bartle Bogle Hegarty /70.2 Courtesy of The Advertising Archives /71.1 Reprint courtesy of Avis. Agency: DDB /71.2 Agency: DDB New York /71.3 Agency: BBDO Duesseldorf /72.1 Courtesy of BBDO Singapore /72.2 Courtesy of Mother London /73.1 Courtesy of The Advertising Archives /73.2 Reprinted by courtesy of Smith Micro Software, Inc. Agency: Saatchi & Saatchi /73.3 Agency: DDB /74.1 Agency: Leo Burnett London /74.2 Reprint courtesy of AB InBev. Courtesy of The Advertising Archives /74.3 Agency: Lowe London /75.1 Agency: Crispin Porter + Bogusky /75.2 Agency: BBH /75.3 The National Gallery, London: The Grand Tour. Agency: The Partners. Art directors: Jim Prior, Greg Quinton. Design Director: Robert Ball. Project managers: Donna Hemley, Andrew Webster. Designers: Kevin Lan, Paul Currah, Jay Lock. Copywriter: Jim Davies. Interactive Agency: Digit /76.1 Agency: Wieden + Kennedy /76.2 Agency: BBH London /76.3 Agency: Arnold /77.1 Agency: Lowe London /77.2 Agency: Saatchi & Saatchi New York /77.3 Agency: M&C Saatchi London /78.1 Courtesy of Del Campo Nazca Saatchi & Saatchi /78.2 Agency: Ogilvy SA /78.3 TBWA London /79.1 Agency: Ogilvy SA /79.2 Agency: CHI & Partners /79.3 Agency: Grabarz & Partner. Managing Creative: Ralf Heuel. Creative Direction: Timm Weber, Gosta Diehl, Oliver Heidorn. Art Direction: Jan Riggert. Graphics: Matthias Khaled Baare. Production: Karlotta Ahrens. Text: Tobias Burger /80.1 Reprint courtesy of Carlsberg. Agency: Saatchi and Saatchi /80.2 Agency: Leagas Delaney UK /80.3 Agency: Saatchi & Saatchi Malaysia /81.1 Courtesy of BBDO Germany GmbH /81.2 Courtesy of Lowe Bull Cape Town /81.3 Courtesy of Del Campo Nazca Saatchi & Saatchi /82.1 Agency: DDB /82.2 Agency: Ogilvy Brazil /82.3 Courtesy of TBWA ESPAÑA /83.1 Agency: Saatchi & Saatchi NZ /83.2 Agency: Boase Massimi Pollitt. Courtesy of The Advertising Archives /84.1 Agency: Callegari Berville Grey /84.2 Agency: Ogilvy & Mather Singapore /84.3 Agency: Delehanty, Kurnit and Geller /85.1 Agency: Saatchi and Saatchi London /85.2 Agency: HHCL. Courtesy of The Advertising Archives /85.3 HHCL. Courtesy of The Advertising Archives /86.1 Agency: Scholz & Friends Berlin /86.3 The Quality Street name and image is reproduced with the kind permission of Société des Produits Nestlé S.A. Agency: Lowe London /87.1 Courtesy of Bensimon Byrne D'Arcy Canada /87.2 Reprint courtesy of IKEA. Agency: St Luke's. Courtesy of The Advertising Archives /87.3 Courtesy of The Advertising Archives /88.2 Agency: a&eDDB, London. Production: Aardman Animations. Photography: Giles Revell /89.1 Agency: Leo Burnett Copenhagen /89.2 Agency: Euro RSCG /89.3 Reprint courtesy of Huntsman Advanced Materials. Agency: FCO Univas /90.1 Agency: Ogilvy and Mather London /90.2 Agency: Fallon London /90.3 Agency: LOWE Howard-Spink / Courtesy of The Advertising Archives /91.1 Agency: Ogilvy and Mather Thailand /91.2 Reprint courtesy of AB InBev /91.3 Agency: AMV /92.1 Courtesy of The Advertising Archives /92.2 Agency: BBH. Courtesy of The Advertising Archives /92.3 Agency: Collett Dickenson Pearce /93.1 Reprint courtesy of the Coca-Cola Company. Agency: Wieden + Kennedy Amsterdam /93.2 Agency: Saatchi and Saatchi /93.3 Agency: Collett Dickenson Pearce /94.1 Agency: Ogilvy and Mather /94.2 Agency: Fallon London /94.3 Agency: BSB Dorland. Courtesy of The Advertising Archives /95.1 Reprint courtesy of Tate Gallery /95.2 Agency: Odiorne Wilde Narraway and Partners London /95.3 Courtesy of Droga5 /96.1 Agency: The Glue Societ. Creatives: Luke Crethar & Matt Devine. Direction: Gary Freedman & Matt Devine /96.2 Agency: Simons Palmer Denton Clemmow and Johnson /96.3 DDB London /97.1 Agency: GGK London /97.2 Agency: DDB /97.3 Agency: DDB /98.1 Agency: AMV BBDO /98.2 Agency: Gilbert Advertising /98.3 Agency: Asher & Partners /99.1 Agency: Cliff Freeman & Partners /99.2 Agency: Scali, McCabe, Sloves /99.3 Agency: HHCL. Courtesy of The Advertising Archives /100.1 Agency: DDB London. Courtesy of The Advertising Archives /100.2 Agency: Cliff Freeman & Partners /100.3 Agency: Crispin Porter + Bogusky.

Author Acknowledgments
I learned about many of these techniques on the West Herts College Copywriting and Art Direction course, which is run by Tony Cullingham. You can find out more about the course at tonycullingham.com Thanks also to Sophie Wise, Sarah Batten, Sophie Drysdale and Ida Riveros.

9/2015